Wired *for* Learning

Wired *for* Learning

Jane Lasarenko

Alverno College
Library Media Center
Milwaukee, Wisconsin

Wired for Learning

Credits

President
Roland Elgey

Title Manager
Kathie-Jo Arnoff

Editorial Services Director
Elizabeth Keaffaber

Managing Editor
Michael Cunningham

Director of Marketing
Lynn E. Zingraf

Acquisitions Manager
Elizabeth South

Senior Product Director
Lisa D. Wagner

Production Editor
Julie A. McNamee

Editors
Lisa M. Gebken
June Waldman
Thomas F. Hayes

Strategic Marketing Manager
Barry Pruett

Product Marketing Manager
Kris Ankney

**Assistant Product
Marketing Managers**
Karen Hagan
Christy M. Miller

Technical Editor
Julie Sykes

Media Development Specialist
David Garratt

Technical Support Specialist
Nadeem Muhammed

Acquisitions Coordinator
Tracy C. Williams

Software Relations Coordinator
Susan Gallagher

Editorial Assistant
Virginia Stoller

Book Designer
Barbara Kordesh

Cover Designer
Jay Corpus

Production Team
Marcia Brizendine
Jason R. Carr
Maribeth Echard
Jessica Ford
Laura Knox

Indexer
Craig A. Small

Composed in *Syntax*, *Times*, and *MCPdigital* by Que Corporation.

To my husband Kim, without whose enthusiasm, help, love, and patience, I couldn't live so well.

About the Author

Jane Lasarenko, Ph.D.

Dr. Lasarenko received her B.A. and M.A. in English from The State University of New York at Binghamton and her Ph.D. from The Ohio State University. Her areas of specialization were Critical Theory and the Novel, but when computers hit the mainstream in education she found another niche. Long a proponent of collaborative and problem-based learning strategies, Dr. Lasarenko has investigated how to incorporate computer technology in her composition and literature classes for the past five years. Dr. Lasarenko is currently living and teaching in the Texas Panhandle.

Acknowledgments

This book is dedicated to all the techno-pioneers, past and present, who have helped me on my path. To the Tuesday Night Cafe regulars go my heartfelt thanks for all the ongoing conversations. My gratitude also goes to Kevin Enger for his graciousness in providing ongoing technical information and support.

We'd Like to Hear from You!

As part of our continuing effort to produce books of the highest possible quality, Que would like to hear your comments. To stay competitive, we *really* want you, as a computer book reader and user, to let us know what you like or dislike most about this book or other Que products.

You can mail comments, ideas, or suggestions for improving future editions to the address below, or send us a fax at (317) 581-4663. For the online inclined, Macmillan Computer Publishing has a forum on CompuServe (type **GO QUEBOOKS** at any prompt) through which our staff and authors are available for questions and comments. The address of our Internet site is **http://www.quecorp.com** (World Wide Web).

In addition to exploring our forum, please feel free to contact me personally to discuss your opinions of this book: I'm **76507,2715** on CompuServe, and I'm **karnoff@que.mcp.com** on the Internet.

Thanks in advance—your comments will help us to continue publishing the best books available on computer topics in today's market.

Kathie-Jo Arnoff
Title Manager
Que Corporation
201 W. 103rd Street
Indianapolis, Indiana 46290
USA

Contents at a Glance

Table of Contents

4 Continuing the Conversations   75

7 "MOOving" Right Along   143

8 And Then Came the Web and It Was Good   183

Introduction

We've come so far from the days of the little red schoolhouse, sitting in our town's main square, its bell ringing several times a day, calling all children to lessons and classes. Our towns now have several schools, not one; our children come from all ethnic and economic backgrounds, but our mission, our calling if you will, has remained the same: to educate our youth and provide them with the tools and skills to be active, literate, and knowledgeable citizens.

Through the years, we have risen to the demands of this mission. Scrutinizing ourselves, our students, and our world, we have been lifelong learners, constantly learning, adapting, and changing our pedagogies and priorities to the needs of our students and the world around us. With new and ever-changing technology, we are now again in the position to learn and use these tools to meet the needs of our students and ourselves.

Why You Need This Book

The past 20 years have witnessed a technological revolution the likes of which hasn't occurred since the invention of the printing press. Seemingly overnight, the world has shrunk considerably. I can communicate with my colleague in Egypt almost immediately; almost as quickly as I send off a message to her, I can get a reply. I've even had "conversations" with colleagues around the globe in "real time," just as if I were on the telephone, at no cost, sitting at my computer. Incredible. Moreover, my ability to do research, to learn more and contribute more to this terrific community of teachers worldwide, has grown astronomically. Sitting here at my computer, I can access a global library of information—any time of day or night.

Make no mistake about it, the greatest information revolution has occurred. And we owe it to ourselves, our students, and our students' students to learn this new technology as quickly as possible. We need to learn how to teach with this technology today and not tomorrow. Our students will grow up in a world very different from our own, and we need to prepare them for it.

This book is designed to help you get started in this new endeavor. I have tried to gear the book and the assignments and projects to all K-12 levels. While most of the projects in this book are designed for grades 7-12, they usually contain variations that will allow you to adapt them to grades K-6 as well. Nonetheless, this book is also useful to teachers at universities, especially since we're all pioneers in this new cyberuniverse and we're all in this together.

It's not easy learning all this newfangled technology; it takes time, patience, and practice. I promise you, however, that the information in this book will help make your journey easier, and hence more exciting, fun, and rewarding, both for you and for your students.

The State of Education Today

It's become a common belief that education is in need of improvement in our country. When was that ever not true? Education is always in need of improvement, no matter how good the teachers and no matter how much money is invested. The future is only as good as the citizenry who mold it, lead it, and live in and for it. And that citizenry is only as good as we teachers that help create it. While I'm no proponent of federal intervention at any level in our schools, I am heartened by the government's current push for better schools and willingness to aid school districts in acquiring technological tools for learning.

Federal and State Mandates and Goals for Education

In 1994, as you may recall, *Goals 2000: Educate America Act* was passed into law. This act provided funds to state and local school districts to support "comprehensive, standards-based improvements in teaching and learning." In 1996, this act was amended and supplemented by the 1996 Technology Initiative, designed to implement President Bill Clinton's statement in his State of the Union address that:

"In our schools, every classroom in America must be connected to the information superhighway, with computers and good software, and well-trained teachers. We are working with the telecommunications industry, educators, and parents to connect 20 percent of California's classrooms this spring, and every classroom and every library in the entire United States by the year 2000. I ask Congress to support this educational technology initiative so that we can make sure this national partnership succeeds."

Vice President Al Gore supplemented this Presidential statement, adding: "By the year 2000, 60 percent of the new jobs in America will require advanced technological skills."

These two federal initiatives challenge us greatly. We need to learn a whole lot more—not only about the pedagogical heuristics we adopt in our classrooms—but about the new technologies and how they can help us implement those classroom strategies. The full text of the 1994 Goals 2000 Act can be found on the U.S. Department of Education home page or at **http://www.ed.gov/G2K/GoalsRpt/**.

How the Internet Will Help Meet These Goals

In 1995, KickStart Initiative, the U.S. Advisory Council on the National Information Infrastructure, found that educational technology has the following benefits:

- Brings the world to the classroom. No matter what their socioeconomic or ethnic background, and no matter where they live, the learning field for all students can be leveled. Students are introduced to people, places, and ideas they might otherwise not be exposed to.

- Enables students to learn by doing. Studies have confirmed what many instinctively knew—that children who are actively engaged in learning learn more. The effects are particularly noticeable among students who were not high achievers under more traditional methods.

- Networked projects, where students work with others and conduct their own research and analysis, can transform students into committed and exhilarated learners.

- Encourages students and parents with limited or no English skills to learn English by engaging them in interactive learning.

- Makes parents partners in their children's education by connecting the school with homes, libraries, or other access ports.

- Makes it possible for educators to teach at more than one location simultaneously. Vastly expands opportunities for students in small, remote areas, linking them to students in more diversely populated urban and suburban areas.

- Enables educators to accommodate the varied learning styles and paces of learning within the classroom. This makes available individualized instruction techniques that are a proven factor in student achievement.

- Encourages students to become lifelong learners who can access, analyze, and synthesize information from a variety of sources.

- Enables administrators and educators to reduce time spent on administration recordkeeping, increasing efficiency so they can spend more time with students.

- Makes students proficient in the basic technological skills needed to take their place in society, whether they enter the working world directly after high school or pursue further formal education.

Note More information about the benefits of information technology for the classroom can be found at the following location: "Educational Technology: Changing Teaching and Learning." KickStart Initiative, U.S. Advisory Council on the National Information Infrastructure. Cited in Educational Technology Home Page:

http://www.whitehouse.gov/edtech.html

These claims are sweeping indeed; moreover, they can hardly be realized without a firm pedagogical grounding. Recent years have seen a resurgence of interest in learning styles and techniques heretofore known but not thoroughly implemented: cooperative, collaborative, and problem-based learning. The Internet demands we investigate and use these learning methods more fully.

Cooperative Learning

As you know, small cooperative learning groups have come back into vogue as a way to enhance student interaction and increase learning of course content material. The Internet can enhance small group learning by broadening the "group" to other students located around the world. Imagine the learning that could occur if your students could form small groups with others from a different part of the county, country, India, China, South America, or Russia.

Until very recently, educators interested in bilingual education or language acquisition skills have used the Internet extensively in their classrooms; now, more and more teachers of social studies and language arts are joining the ranks of educators making the world a much smaller place. Math and science teachers are also starting to investigate ways that the Internet can help their students join with others around the globe.

Collaborative Learning

We've known for quite some time that active and engaged students are learning more and faster than those who are passive. The Internet enables collaborative learning projects in ways heretofore only imagined. Using Internet technology will allow your students to engage in writing and learning projects with others from around the world, not just with students in the classroom.

Moreover, the outcomes or results of these collaborative student projects can be "published" for the rest of the world to see! All of a sudden, students have a real audience and a real purpose for their work. Students worldwide can visit your students' collaborative projects and comment upon them, learn from them, and extend them.

Problem-Based Learning

Problem-based learning (PBL) is another pedagogical heuristic that's been revitalized through the use of computer technology and the Internet. The Internet can never replace the classroom experience of group efforts to solve problems; however, students are able to discuss aspects of the problem with others from far away, and they have a world of information at their fingertips.

Distance Learning

We are truly at the beginning of a revolution in how and where we learn. As cited previously, the KickStart Initiative found that technology "makes it possible for educators to teach at more than one location simultaneously." What with video and satellite technology, computer synchronous and asynchronous conferencing capability, and with the information possible to be accessed and retrieved by students everywhere, we are on the brink of radical changes in our education delivery capability. These changes can benefit students in remote geographical areas as well as home-schooled children.

What This Book Contains

This book is designed to help you get started using technology in your classes. It is not meant as a "how to" book on using computers, but rather as a "how to teach" with the technology. Every chapter contains a narrative portion dealing with the use of the technology as an aid to cooperative or collaborative learning, a how-to section on using the software programs that enable you to connect to the Internet, an assignment section providing exercises to help your students learn to use the technology, and a projects section that provides detailed large projects for your classes to share with other classes from around the world.

A detailed, chapter-by-chapter preview follows:

Chapter 1, "So What's the Big Deal About This Inter-What?," provides a brief overview of the Internet and its technologies and programs.

Chapter 2, "Accessing Information: A World of Information at Your Fingertips," provides detailed information about doing research on the Internet with Telnet, Gopher, and text-only software.

Chapter 3, "Communicating Faster, Cheaper, and Farther," provides detailed explanations and information about e-mail, what you and your classes can do with it, and ways to contact other K-12 teachers around the world.

Chapter 4, "Continuing the Conversations," furthers the discussion about e-mail and provides information about creating, joining, and using listservs and USENET newsgroups in your classroom.

Chapter 5, "Just Connect," introduces the concepts of computer networks and how to use them in your classroom.

Chapter 6, "Conversing with the World," discusses chat technology and explains how to join other teachers and classes in a chatroom.

Chapter 7, "'MOOving' Right Along," provides detailed instructions and information about MOOs and MUDs, from setting up your virtual classroom on a MOO to meeting with classes from around the world in a virtual environment.

Chapter 8, "And Then Came the Web and It Was Good," provides basic information about the World Wide Web and navigating through it. Instructions about creating your own HTML multimedia pages are included as well.

Appendix A, "Glossary of Terms," provides basic definitions and explanations of all Internet terminology.

Appendix B, "Academic Listservs and USENET Groups," provides information about subscribing to academic listservs and USENET newsgroups in your subject area.

Appendix C, "Education Resources on the World Wide Web," is designed to help you find information on the WWW related to teaching with technology. This appendix provides annotated descriptions of some of the best K-12 sites on the Web.

Appendix D, "A Gallery of Projects on the World Wide Web," provides information about existing K-12 home pages and Web sites with some pictures to help you design your own Web projects and pages.

How to Use This Book

I've tried to organize this book to make it as easy for both experienced users and novices as possible. The book is loosely organized by technologies, going from the simplest to the most complex. The first chapter should be read by novices—those who may know what the Internet is but have little direct experience using it. Those familiar with the technologies may consider going to individual chapters as they like.

Each chapter is divided into the following broad areas: a narrative that discusses the use of the technology in the classroom, a "how-to" section covering the software, an exercise section designed to help students master the technologies, and a project section that provides step-by-step instructions for starting and implementing major, collaborative projects.

> **Note** This book uses software and screen shots of programs designed for use with Windows 95. Those of you working on other platforms or with other software will notice some slight variations in the instructions or screen shots. These variations are insignificant in terms of using the information in this book. You can use this book, the projects, and the ideas regardless of what kind of computer you have—as long as you have the proper network and Internet connections.

Where you start in a chapter is up to you; if you know the software, you might be interested in hearing about my experiences with teaching with the technology. Or, you might want to jump in and take a look at the possible projects you could have your students work on.

What chapter you choose to begin with is again up to you; if you're like me and can't wait to get students "hooked on learning" through the World Wide Web, start with Chapter 8, "And Then Came the Web and It Was Good."

If you're familiar with e-mail already, consider starting with Chapter 4, "Continuing the Conversations," to get information about how you can hook your students up with others around the globe. As with any new learning experience, start where you're most comfortable.

Whatever you do, *don't* try to implement all these new strategies at once. Go slowly, and see how each one works for you and your class. Remember—all new things take time and patience. Make sure you have alternative lesson plans for each "technoclass" you want to teach. You never know when the computers may break down, or your students decide they really don't want to mess with computers that day.

This book covers all the current basic Internet technologies, but please note that they'll be changing even as you begin trying these out. To help us adapt to these new technologies, to keep us current with potential changes, and to allow us to collaborate and share our experiences, this book is supported with an online site. The address is **http://www.quecorp.com/wired**. Visit our Web site often for updates and help. The times, they are a-changin'! Enjoy.

So What's the Big Deal About This Inter-What?

Sneak Peek

- A Very Brief History of the Internet
- Preparing for Battle
- Amassing the Forces
- Connecting the Players to the Playing Field
- Arming Yourself as a Cyberwarrior

Once upon a time, long ago and far away, there was a woman. A woman who was somewhat brighter than most, but more important, far more curious and impetuous. She also, by the way, had a terrible memory. Every day, she would get up to check on her stores of food for her family; no matter how hard she tried, she just couldn't remember what she had left over. Everyone complained about how much time she wasted recounting everything every morning. One day, when particularly befuddled, she couldn't even remember what she had counted! She took a lot of teasing over that one. Feeling saddened by her friends' laughter, and at her wits' end, she picked up a rock and made a mark in the ground for every one of each item she had on hand. Then, when she used a particular item, she removed a mark from the ground. And for a long time after that people continued to scoff at her method for remembering.

About 45 years ago, millennia after that technology foremother, another person decided that universities would be vastly improved if faculty could communicate with one another much more quickly. Important work was being done all over the world, but finding out about that work took a whole lot of time. Consequently, there was a lot of duplication of efforts—duplication that again wasted precious time in making progress and discoveries. What if people could share their work and information almost immediately?

And so began the Internet.

A Very Brief History of the Internet

The history of the Internet (Net) begins in the 1960s at the U.S. Defense Department's Advanced Research Projects Agency (ARPA). Their mission was to create a communications system with no obvious central control point and the ability of all surviving points to reestablish contact in the event of an attack on any one point.

From Small Beginnings...

In 1969, the first ARPANET Information Message Processor (IMP) was installed at UCLA. Additional IMPs were soon installed at Stanford Research Institute (SRI), the University of California at Santa Barbara (UCSB), and the University of Utah. The research that allowed these three machines to "talk" to one another was the beginning of what is now the Internet.

An "internet" is a connected set of networks using Transmission Control Protocol (TCP) and Internet Protocol (IP). Most computers use these protocols together, and so you'll often hear that you need to set up your computer with TCP/IP. The Internet is nothing more than the collection of computers connected with one another via TCP/IP.

In the 1970s and early 1980s, another kind of network technology was developed: one that allowed scientists and scholars to communicate on a daily basis—e-mail (see Chapter 4).

E-Mail Arrives!

The 1970s saw the birth and explosive growth of the home computer, the PC. Personal computers were every bit as powerful as the early large mainframes, and *modems* became more powerful and more affordable, thus allowing people to connect to computers at work.

TECH TALK **Modem:**
A device that connects your computer to a telephone line which, in turn, connects to another modem on a remote computer.

These early technologies account for the phenomenon we now call the Internet.

Conferencing and Networking

As time passed, the technology of electronic mail systems was extended to what we now call conferencing. Computer conferencing is two-way and one-to-many communication. Again, as the technology developed, this conferencing grew to include asynchronous and synchronous capabilities.

TECH TALK **Asynchronous:**
Not at the same time.

TECH TALK **Synchronous:**
At the same time.

Examples of asynchronous conferencing are e-mail and USENET news-groups (see Chapter 4). Synchronous conferencing is generally done through chatrooms (Chapter 6) and MOOs (Chapter 7).

Preparing for Battle

While the current administration is pushing technology development in the school system and providing numerous grants and funding support, there is still a great deal of resistance by school administrators, not to mention parents. As with anything new, people are suspicious about the usefulness of all this "newfangled" technology in teaching. And they're right to be suspicious; the startup costs for computer network capability are very high. Since you've purchased this book, I assume you're interested in helping your school get "wired" or, if you already have a computer classroom in place, in helping your fellow educators and students become more technoliterate. So you need to arm yourself with some basic information as you start to talk to your school administrators and community.

First and foremost, you need to arm yourself with a sound plan, one that includes detailed pedagogical goals. You cannot convince technology-suspicious administrators to support expensive technologies without making your instructional goals very clear. You must show them that computer-mediated communication is not just "typing," or worse, "playing." It helps to have some marketing information as well, such as a short bibliography or a small set of professional publications that encourage technology practices in the classroom. If you know of a school in your area that has a networked lab, try to set up a demonstration of a technology-assisted class you would teach. Few people can resist the sheer fun of learning in that environment. If you still meet with a good deal of resistance, try to enlist the aid of the larger community.

Amassing the Forces

Most institutions connected to the Internet extend that connection to their entire computer network: offices, computer rooms, and even classrooms that are sufficiently equipped. This extended connection allows the users of the local network of a campus or organization to not only communicate with one another, but also to conduct exchanges with users and organizations outside of their own. The first thing that will take place when your school is ready to be connected to the Internet is your school's computer science folks will assign everyone a unique account composed of a username and a password.

Equipment Alert

As you already know, the world is currently divided between two main species of computer: Macintoshes (Apple) and PCs (IBM and IBM-like spinoffs). Either of these computer platforms is fine; the applications described in this book work with both kinds of machines. You need to be aware, however, that what you see on your own computer screen may not match the diagrams and pictures in this book exactly. Programs look different on every machine—sometimes even on two different machines of the same type! These individual variations are found throughout the cyber-universe, just as they are found in the natural world.

 **Username:**
A unique, personal identifier, often consisting of your first initial and your last name. My username is "jlasarenko."

Password:
A unique combination of letters, numbers, and typographic symbols that protects your safety when logging in to a server. No one but you should know your password.

Your school's computer technology staff will probably take care of just about everything needed to connect you and your classroom to the Internet. You can recognize them quite easily: They're the ones who walk around hurriedly, faces down, muttering strange incantations and magic phrases. They're hard to talk to as well, seeming to have a language unique to themselves. Yet a little basic knowledge will allow you to "interface" (computerese for communicate or interact) with them fairly successfully.

Connecting the Players to the Playing Field

Communicating with your technical support staff isn't terribly difficult; it just requires a little knowledge of computer terminology. Computers are wonderful machines, capable of storing a great deal more information than we can—even in a library. They can also search for information a lot more quickly than we. But one computer sitting alone on a desk, as wonderful as it may be, is insufficient. It (and we) need to be able to "talk" to other computers to obtain information we need.

A "network" is nothing more than two or more computers connected together via a cable or telephone.

When you connect two computers in this manner, one computer gets designated as the "master computer" and the other as the "slave computer," as shown in Figure 1.1. All this means is that one computer acts as the server or host for the second computer. When you connect many computers in this manner, you have an "intranet."

An intranet is really quite similar to the Internet. Picture a number of computers linked together in a classroom, which is, in turn, linked with a classroom in another part of the building. These two linked classrooms form an intranet of sorts. If you link these classrooms with classrooms in other buildings at your campus, you have a genuine intranet—a series of linked local area networks. The "Internet" is nothing more than the aggregate collection of numerous linked intranets, although it is shortly becoming synonymous with the World Wide Web.

Intranets are ideal vehicles for education institutions. For example, while I really want my students to learn how to write for the World Wide Web (see Chapter 8), I don't always want to put their work on display to the world. Having a campus intranet is ideal and provides the best of both worlds: Your students can write Web documents and "publish" them on a campus intranet for your education community, but the rest of the world won't be able to see their work.

Fig. 1.1 Creating a network of connected computers.

The connections between and among the computers are cables called ethernet cables. These cables move (or transport) data from one machine to another. All of the computers in a networked room are then connected via a cable to a server computer in your technical support area. This main computer usually has a direct connection to the Internet via what's called a T-1 connection (another kind of cable).

The same principle holds true if you try to connect to the Internet from home; the difference is that you use a telephone line instead of a direct cable to make the connection. If you want to connect your home computer to the Internet, you need to make special arrangements to do so, either with an Internet Service Provider (ISP) such as America Online, Prodigy, or CompuServe, or with your school's technical support staff. For example, I can connect to the Internet from home by telephoning in to my campus computer via a modem. A modem is a piece of equipment that allows me to send information from my computer across the telephone lines. Once connected to the computer at school, I can access the Internet just as if I were directly connected to it at school.

One important piece of software that is required for a "dial-up" Internet connection (one made via a telephone and modem) is called a "TCP/IP stack." Trumpet Winsock is popular among Windows users for use as a TCP/IP stack, and Windows 95 is packaged with its own. What a TCP/IP stack is exactly isn't that important, just think of it as a kind of "middleman" between the Internet and your computer's application programs.

Arming Yourself as a Cyberwarrior

The application programs that you choose can greatly enhance your experiences on the Net. Students can submit papers over the Net without having to get out in the rain and snow. Classes in one part of the world can interact with another. Information on any topic can be found. But, without the right software, none of these miracles can come to pass.

The most versatile application you need to obtain is a browser such as Netscape or Internet Explorer. A browser is a program that allows you to "browse" the Internet, most often the World Wide Web. Of all the Internet applications, you will probably log the most virtual miles using your World Wide Web browser. It is your window to the world of information.

Browsers are designed to interpret specially coded documents called "Web pages," written in HyperText Markup Language (HTML). These documents contain not only information, but also links that reference other documents that may be selected with a click of the mouse. Clicking a link will cause the browser to look up and load what is referenced, usually another Web page with more links! Browsers are very versatile in their capability as they not only interpret the HTML of Web pages, but are able to handle communications with older methods of information access such as ftp and gopher, which will be discussed in Chapter 2.

Netscape, a very popular browser offered free to educational institutions, is a graphical browser that allows you to see images and pictures. Other browsers are text-only browsers such as Lynx and gopher (see Chapter 2). Text-only browsers are faster and more reliable than graphical browsers; nonetheless, you lose a great deal these days by not being able to see and exploit the multimedia capabilities of the Internet.

Moreover, many browsers are being further developed to handle other applications such as e-mail and newsreader capabilities. Thus, instead of having separate programs to perform every task, you can use one program to perform many! Using a browser such as Netscape saves you time when searching for information and certainly cuts down on the amount of time you need to train students on how to perform tasks.

A full-featured electronic mail program is essential to your being able to compose, send, and receive e-mail. If you have the luxury to choose what you use, choose carefully. Not only will you want to send simple text, but you eventually will want to send other kinds of files, such as graphics and sound files as well. Make sure that the mail program that you use is able to send, receive, and decode attachments. "Attachments" are files of any type that can ride "piggyback" on e-mail from one user to another. You can be sure that your e-mail program can handle attachments if it is MIME-compliant. MIME is a method for exchanging various (text and non-text) file formats.

You may also want to get a newsreader if the browser that you choose doesn't support newsgroups, or you don't like the way that it handles them. Newsgroups comprise a section of the Internet known as USENET. USENET is a collection of discussion groups with a readership that extends worldwide. Users of USENET post articles to groups where they may be read and replied to by others. There are more than 20,000 different topics currently listed in the discussion group index, so you should be able to find something that suits your needs.

You should be warned that "unmoderated" is the operating word when it comes to USENET, where you can find all manner of sordid material, from political hate messages to explicit pornography. Because it operates without any central authority or censor, you may have to assume this role if you find that material nonconducive to a learning environment is finding its way in. Detailed information about e-mail and newsgroups is contained in chapters 3 and 4.

Writing electronic mail, Web browsing, and reading newsgroups comprise the largest majority of Web activity. Arming yourself with programs that perform these functions should set you well on the way to discovering the things that you find most useful on the Internet. A few other single purpose applications may also be useful, such as telnet, gopher, archie, and ftp programs. The uses of these applications are discussed in Chapter 2.

After you become familiar with the basic set of Internet applications, you might want to explore some of the fancier varieties. Some applications available now allow you to conduct voice conversations, others allow you to collaborate with other users online in the creation of a shared document. The list of programs and possibilities grows longer every day. A good collection of Internet applications can be found at TUCOWS, The Ultimate Collection Of Windows Software. These programs are either free or available for a small fee. Their address is **http://tucows.phoenix.net**.

You have just about finished assembling your arsenal in preparation for your Internet epic. You've got your mail reader and your browser and your newsreader. You're set, right? Yes. Well, almost. You may find that you will need to acquire some utility programs to help make life a little easier. For example, many of the files that you will receive from the Net have been compressed, and will need to be expanded before they can be used. Compression is a method of both reducing file size and packing multiple files together into a single unit for ease of storage and transfer. Several schemes of compression are out there, but luckily only a couple of the formats are used widely. You may already be familiar with PKZIP, the most popular file compression utility. You will need to obtain a copy of the right compression utility if you want to be able to use the compressed files that you receive from the Net.

A Look Both Ways

So far, this brief introduction to computers, networks, and the Internet may be helpful and interesting (I hope), but you're probably wondering about how all these technological issues relate to your teaching. The next chapter begins our exploration of ways to use this new technology in our classrooms and discusses the advantages of this technology for your students.

Accessing Information: A World of Information at Your Fingertips

Sneak Peek

- Clients and Servers and Bears, Oh My
- The Wonderful World of Telnet
- Gopher the Gold!
- Finding Information with Veronica
- Jughead
- Searching with Archie
- FTP: "I've gotta ftp…"
- Exploration Assignments:

  2.1: Exploring Gopherspace

  2.2: Searching with Veronica

  2.3: Archie and FTP

- Inter-Netiquette

It's the information that you're after, right? That information is sitting happily on a computer somewhere, free for the taking if you could just find it. Imagine having the world's library at your fingertips; that's what the following research tools provide.

The Internet is a giant collection of information. So many files are out there that it's difficult to keep track of them, even by using computers. Various tools have been created to keep track of files and their locations so they can be accessed quickly and easily.

The tools for information research and retrieval from the Net focus on searching and transferring documents and files. A good Web browser, such as Netscape (see Chapter 8), is the most commonly used tool, since it is able to perform the functions of both ftp and gopher as well as browse World Wide Web (WWW) documents. Web browsers make searching through the menus and directories of gopher and ftp much easier because the menus are usually presented graphically and only require a point and click to get where you want to go. Web browsers take a lot of the work out of the process by performing many of the commands for you, thus saving a lot of typing.

If for some reason you don't have a Web browser, you may have to resort to doing things like they did back in the "olden days" of a few years ago and use tools like telnet, ftp, archie, and gopher. Even with a browser, you might choose to use these tools directly; they're generally much faster than a browser to retrieve information from the Internet.

Clients and Servers and Bears, Oh My

Computers that are connected to the Internet assume one of two roles: client or server. As you might have guessed, a server is a machine that is always connected to the Internet and set up to serve files. A client is a computer that receives the information and is able to interpret it.

Jargon Alert!

The programs that run on a local computer and are used to access information from a remote site are also called clients. A Web browser, such as Netscape, is a client program that is used to receive and interpret http documents. Other types of clients exist for other functions, such as telnet, ftp, and gopher. In order to use those functions, your local machine may require that you run the appropriate client program.

The Wonderful World of Telnet

At one time, telnet was *the* way for computers to connect to one another, mainly for remote users on small computers to connect to mainframes. In fact, the name itself reflects what this program does: You *tele*phone a computer on the Inter*net*. Telnet is generally used in two ways. First, many online databases allow telnet access. You connect to the remote computer and search the database for information you need.

The other way telnet is used is to connect to a remote computer to use the programs that reside on it. For example, let's say you wanted to use a program called gopher (discussed later in this chapter) but you didn't have that program on your computer. You could telnet to a computer that has the program and use its gopher program.

If you should happen to be caught without a browser, you should be able to do just about anything using telnet. Most Internet services, especially the ones discussed in this chapter, can be used through a telnet connection, and WWW documents can even be browsed (to a very limited degree) using a text-based browser such as Lynx.

Like most of the other tools discussed in this chapter, to use telnet you will need to have a telnet client—a software program that runs on your machine while you are connected to the Internet. Many telnet clients exist for just about every type of machine imaginable, so locating one should not be much of a problem. If you happen to be using Windows 95, a telnet client is included with it. All you need to do is click the Run command in the Start menu and type **telnet**.

Remember that although browsers can handle such things as ftp and gopher, telnet is a little bit different, and requires its own client. Most browsers have a preference section that indicates where a telnet client is stored on the computer.

Time to Make a New Connection

Connecting to another machine using telnet usually follows the same procedure no matter where you're trying to connect. When contacted, the remote system (the server) will prompt the user for a login and then a password:

    Connected...
    login:

The thing to keep in mind is that when you log in to a remote machine, you often do not have an account on it—it will not recognize the username and password that you used to log in to your personal account. Most computers require that you have a special telnet account (a login name and password) to access the machine.

Public access machines, however, are set up with special login names and passwords that allow access to certain services by the general public. Most often, you'll see that the login name for general access is "anonymous" and that the password is "guest." Try these if the machine you connect to prompts you for a login and password. (Often, the program on the remote computer is set up to enter these for you.)

To connect to the remote computer, you need to have the domain name or IP address of that machine. These addresses can be obtained from your technical support staff or, in the case of Internet databases, from your reference librarian. Once you have the name or number of the system that you want to connect to, you are ready to begin.

Searching a Database Through Telnet

Let's say you needed to look for some information about the World Wide Web and its connection to education. The first place you might think of looking is in ERIC. You're at home, the weather's bad, and you don't feel like traveling to the campus library. The first thing you'll do, then, is dial into your school's Internet service (or to your own Internet service provider). After you have established a connection to the Internet, open up your telnet program.

In this example, I telnetted to FirstSearch, one of OCLC's many database services. After I connected to that remote computer, it asked me to provide an authorized user number and password that I had obtained from our library. After verifying that I was authorized to use that service, the screen shown in Figure 2.1 came up.

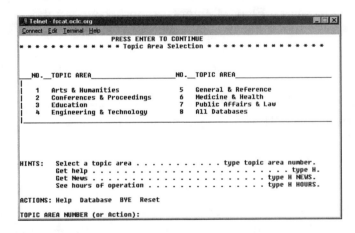

Fig. 2.1   Searching the OCLC Database.

Because I happened to know that the ERIC database is located under "Education," I typed that number when prompted and waited until the next screen appeared (see Figure 2.2).

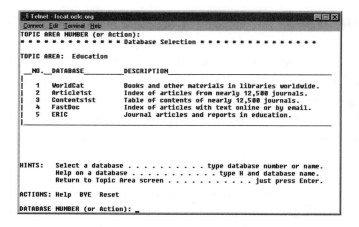

Fig. 2.2 Accessing the ERIC Database.

As you can see, five databases appear under the "Education" category. Because I want to search ERIC, I enter the appropriate number at the prompt and press Enter.

The ERIC database is now available for my search (see Figure 2.3).

As you can see from the figure, the correct way to enter a subject search is to type **su:<*searchterm*>**. Thus, to search for information about the World Wide Web, I typed

> **su:WWW**

and pressed Enter. Notice that there is no space between the colon and the search term. Entering this search command retrieved the information shown in Figure 2.4.

It takes a little practice to become comfortable using telnet. Just remember that it is a program that takes the commands you type on your home computer and sends them to a computer in another location. When that computer receives those commands, it executes them.

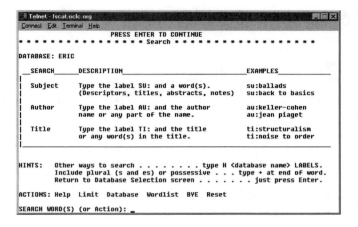

Fig. 2.3 Searching the ERIC Database.

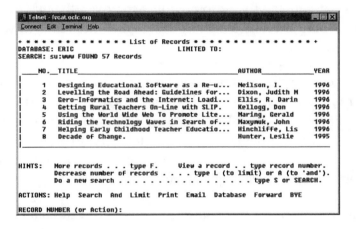

Fig. 2.4 Results of an ERIC subject search.

A Record of Your Journey

There's one more thing to do when starting a telnet session: Start a log file. A *log file* (or capture file) is a transcript of the session that is written to your disk drive. Even if you only use it temporarily and then erase it, create one! Sometimes information scrolls by too fast and you need to look at it again later. Most telnet programs allow you to log a session by activating that feature in its Preferences menu.

Gopher the Gold!

It doesn't seem like you could do anything serious using a tool named *gopher*, but the name has a history behind it. First of all, that is what the program does—it will "go for" information. Moreover, the mascot of the University of Minnesota where the original gopher program was written is—you guessed it—a gopher.

Although its popularity is waning in the face of flashier graphical search tools, gopher is still an excellent method for browsing for information. In some cases, I have found what I was looking for a lot faster through gopher than by trying to wade through the 1.5 million hits returned from a browser search engine. Gopher is very straightforward in its operation; it is a menu of menus, known collectively as gopherspace.

Keep in mind that the items in a gopher menu are just titles, and not the actual documents. Gopher is an excellent tool to use when you don't have a specific file in mind, but need to see what information exists in general. There isn't much required to navigate a gopher menu; simply select a numbered topic on the list and you'll be presented with a new list; choose and select another topic, and a new list will appear, and so on.

Searching Gopherspace

Rather than wandering down the myriad halls and corridors in the maze of gopherspace, you can save some time by conducting a search. Tools have been created for this purpose: Veronica and Jughead.

"Veronica" is an acronym for "Very Easy Rodent-Oriented Net-wide Index to Computerized Archives." The rodent is gopher of course, and veronica will allow you to search through all of gopherspace for a topic of interest. Veronica is accessed through a gopher service and usually appears as a choice on your opening gopher menu (see Figure 2.5).

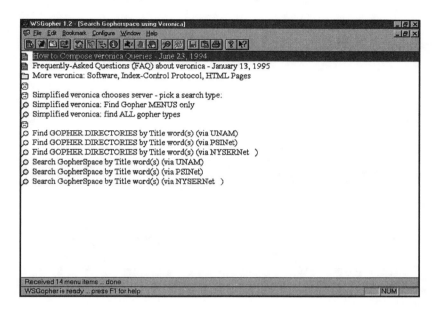

Fig. 2.5   Searching Gopherspace with Veronica.

Veronica will search through either the Titles in gopherspace specifically, or just the Menus, depending on what you select (see Figures 2.6 and 2.7). Veronica will *not* search through the actual text of the documents. Keep in mind that Menu headings are usually more generic than the subjects that they contain. A menu search for "tabby" may not return any results from a menu search, whereas a menu search for "cat" will.

Zen and the Art of Searching

Doing a search is something of an art form. It can sometimes be quite a challenge to find a document. Sometimes it helps to go from the general to the specific, sometimes vice versa. Knowing exactly what keywords you need to use and how to phrase them to a search program comes with experience.

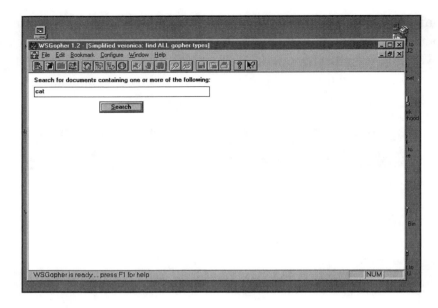

Fig. 2.6   Searching with Veronica.

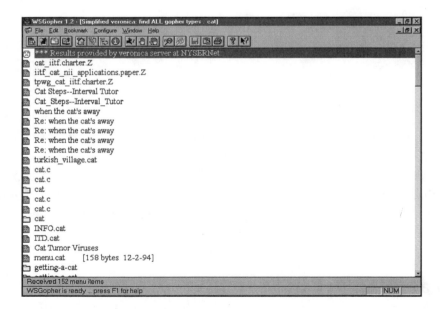

Fig. 2.7   Results of a Veronica Search.

You will probably want to begin with simple keywords for a search. Most systems interpret multiple keywords to mean that you want documents that contain all of them. You can use the word "and" between your keywords, which means the same thing. The words "or" and "not" also have special meaning to most search engines. With them you can specify elaborate search phrases such as:

meat and potatoes not quiche or spinach

If things get very complicated, use () parentheses to help the searcher understand better:

(meat and potatoes) not (quiche or spinach)

The browser will interpret this search request as follows: Go out into gopherspace and retrieve all document references that contain both the words "meat" and "potatoes," then search those documents and give me only those that do not contain the words "quiche" or "spinach."

Tip for Success Be careful about what terms you use for a search. You can easily get overwhelmed with replies to your query, especially when you use OR. Try to avoid terms like "text" or "Internet," or you might byte off more than you can chew!

Narrowing the Field

You can narrow your search by specifying file types as well. Gopher document listings are coded according to type. Table 2.1 provides gopher document numeric codes:

Table 2.1   Gopher Document File-Type Codes

Code	Description
0	Text File
1	Directory

continues

Table 2.1   Continued

Code	Description
2	CSO name server
4	Mac HQX file
5	PC binary
7	Full Text Index (gopher menu)
8	telnet Session
9	Binary File
s	Sound
e	Event (not in 2.06)
i	Image (other than GIF)
m	MIME multipart/mixed message
t	TN3270 Session
c	Calendar (not in 2.06)
g	GIF image
h	HTML, HyperText Markup Language

If you are seeking only a certain type of file, you can specify what you want by typing **-t** (for the type) after the keyword. If you want only images of cats, don't use **cat** and **image** for keywords, use **cat -ti** instead.

Jughead

An accomplice to Veronica is Jughead. Jughead is an acronym for "Jonzy's Universal Gopher Hierarchy Excavation And Display." It also allows searches of gopher menus from a maintained index.

The titles returned from a search will probably be confusing at first, but soon you'll realize (for the most part) what they mean. You'll be able to recognize and avoid library book catalog listings and replies ("Re:") from USENET newsgroups if you are more interested in another kind of file.

Searching with Archie

Files are stored on remote servers in an archive. This is where the term "archie" comes from—short for archive. Unlike gopher, archie is a search tool for finding a particular file or document. Although its use is a little more complex, with a little practice, using archie can be a quick, convenient way of locating an archive that contains the file you are after.

Archie was started as a file databasing project by the computer science department at McGill University. It was so successful that it began to be adopted by other sites on the Internet, who cooperate to keep their databases updated. Updates are made at least monthly, so the information that you find shouldn't be too stale, but you may not be able to find last week's latest release of a version of software. Archie servers, like everything else, have moved into the world of hypertext, and are referred to as archieplexes.

After you have a logged into an archie server, or host, don't forget to start a log file for the session. You will be presented with the command prompt on your screen:

```
archie>
```

Now it's time to tell archie what information you're looking for. If you were, say, trying to research Beowulf, and you wanted to find a public domain translation of it, you would type

archie> find beowulf

which will return a list with entries like the following:

```
Host wcarchive.cdrom.com    (165.113.58.253)
Last updated 03:13 17 Sep 1996
   Location: /.22/obi/Anglo-Saxon
      FILE   -r—r—r—  147140 bytes  15:00  9 Jul 1993
Beowulf.Translated.Gunmere
```

Note Archie cannot give you the actual file, just a list of the locations where you can find it. You'll need a program called ftp (discussed later in this chapter) to get the file. To get a copy of a file, have the Host and Location information ready, because you'll need it when you use ftp.

Like gopher, archie requires a client on the local computer, but you can always use telnet to get to a site. The familiar login: prompt should appear, and the response is generally the word *archie*; sometimes it is *guest*, but the system itself should tell you what it expects you to enter.

Searching with Lynx

Should you find yourself in the unenviable position of having to search for and examine HTML documents without a graphical Web browser, a way does exist: lynx. Lynx is a text-based browser that can be used through a telnet session to interpret hypertext documents. Of course, lynx doesn't display graphics, and is of limited functionality, but if you must—use it!

Lynx uses the arrow keys at the bottom of your computer keyboard for navigation. In lynx, the right arrow selects a choice; the left arrow brings you back to the previous screen.

FTP: "I've gotta ftp..."

The majority of activity on the Internet involves the transfer of files. To expedite matters, an entire tool has been created for nothing but this purpose: the file transfer protocol, or ftp. Ftp takes a little getting used to, and takes a little more typing than using a browser such as Netscape, but it has some advantages that a browser doesn't.

Opening a Connection

The first thing you need before doing an ftp session is a site to connect to. This is most likely an address returned from an archie search. After you have a place in mind, you can open a connection to it. This is another case where your computer needs to have its own ftp program running, which is available for most computers. One is supplied with Windows 95; simply type **ftp** in the Start, Run menu or from a DOS command line.

After you get the ftp> prompt, you are ready to begin. You need to "open" a session with the machine that you want to reach:

    ftp> open wcarchive.cdrom.com

The address part is either the Internet name of the host you're connecting to, like ftp.something.com, or a number like 165.113.58.253 (the IP number). The screen will look something like Figure 2.8.

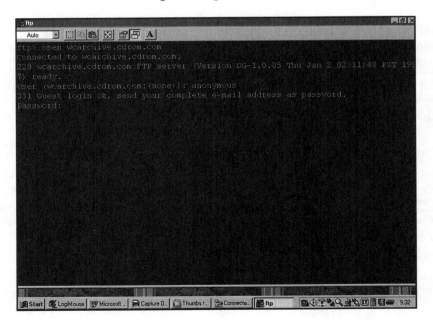

Fig. 2.8 A typical ftp session.

You start out in the root directory of the system that you have connected to. It's the top of an upside-down tree that you need to navigate along to find the branch that contains the data you want. It will most likely be a UNIX directory, so some of the names might look weird. You won't need to go searching around through all the directories, because you have the location from the archie search or some other source. For the most part, however, most servers place the available files in the /pub directory.

When using ftp, you'll mainly be doing three things: changing to the directory that the file you need is in, listing the files inside a directory, and getting the file. The following example shows how to retrieve a file named "Beowulf Translated Gunmere" from the Anglo-Saxon subdirectory of a server. First, you need to change to the correct subdirectory. The command for changing directories is cd:

        cd /.22/obi/Anglo-Saxon

If the directory names are very long, you might consider changing directories in small increments, since you may have to retype the whole thing if you make a mistake:

        cd .22
        cd obi
        cd Anglo-Saxon

To back up a level to where you were before, type "**cd ..**" and be sure to include the space between the ".." and the "cd."

You can always find out what directory you are in by using the print working directory ("pwd") command.

> **Tip for Success** Notice the foreslash ("/") before pub. DOS uses a backslash ("\") to separate directories; UNIX uses a foreslash to separate the names of subdirectories.

Now you need to find out what files are in the subdirectory. You can get a title-only listing by typing **ls**. For more information, try **ls -l**, which will display a listing with directory and date information:

```
150 Opening ASCII mode data connection for /bin/ls.
total 2802
drwxr-xr-x  2 root  wheel     512 Jul 23 01:15 ASC
drwxr-xr-x  2 root  wheel     512 Jul 23 01:14 Anglo-Saxon.Chronicles
drwxr-xr-x  2 root  wheel     512 Nov 16  1995 Beowulf
-r--r--r--  1 root  wheel  147140 Jul  9 1993
Beowulf.Translated.Gunmere
drwxr-xr-x  2 root  wheel     512 Nov 16  1995
Beowulf.Translated.Harvard.Classics
drwxr-xr-x  2 root  wheel    1024 Nov 16  1995 Folio.Images
-r--r--r--  1 root  wheel    2714 Mar  2 1994 Humorous
-r--r--r--  1 root  wheel     905 Feb 17 1994 Not.Beowulf
drwxr-xr-x  2 root  wheel    8192 Nov 16  1995 aspr
-r--r--r--  1 root  wheel  616308 Aug 10 1994 aspr.tar.gz
-r--r--r--  1 root  wheel  616314 Aug 10 1994 aspr1.tar.gz
```

The file listings that start with a "d" are really directories. You can explore them using cd and cd .. to move around.

Retrieving a File via FTP

Now that you've found the file you're looking for, it's time to retreive it. The command to retrieve a file is **get**. Here's how it works:

get <*filename*>

You need to be in the same directory that the file is in, or type the entire directory path to the file.

Note The most important thing to remember before you get a file is to be in BINary, or image mode. Usually when you log into a server, you start out in ASCII mode. ASCII mode is fine for plain text files, but it *does not work* for compressed files, which will not uncompress properly if transferred in ASCII mode. To get into binary mode, type **bin** at the > prompt.

```
ftp> bin
200 Type set to I.
ftp> get Beowulf.Translated.Gunmere
200 PORT command successful.
150 Opening BINARY mode data connection for
Beowulf.Translated.Gunmere (147140 bytes).
226 Transfer complete.
147140 bytes received in 26.58 seconds (5.54 Kbytes/sec)
ftp>
```

One advantage to using an ftp client program instead of a browser is that you are able to get multiple files, using mget.

```
mget *.*
```

Be careful about using mget; you can sometimes get so many files that you accidentally fill up your disk drive. As in DOS, *.* represents every file in the directory; thus, **mget b*.*** would get every file starting with the letter "b."

If you ever need to, the commands **put** and **mput** will put files from your computer onto the remote host, but you'll need to have access privileges.

When you have finished retrieving the files, it is time to close the session using the **close** command, or you can simply type **bye**. If you used the **close** command to end your current ftp session, type **quit** to exit the program.

Recognizing the Kind of File You Retrieved

Computer files come in a huge number of flavors, with different types and formats. Some files may be graphics, others text, others executable programs. A majority of the files on the Net have been compressed for storage and transfer purposes. Many people are familiar with .ZIP files, which have been compressed using PKZIP.EXE.

Several methods of compression exist, each with its own file type. Aside from .ZIP files, .ARJ and .LZH files are popular, and you are bound to come across files with strange looking extensions such as .TAR as well as .z, .Gz, and .Z. These last four are UNIX format files. This doesn't mean that you can't use the information inside of them on a DOS machine; you'll simply need some file utilities to uncompress them. As you become more experienced on the Internet, you will probably collect some utility programs for uncompressing and viewing files.

Quick and Easy UNIX Command Reference

The world of UNIX can be somewhat daunting at first. Table 2.2 gives you a few commands that will help you make it through the wilds of this cryptic universe. All UNIX commands should be entered in lowercase. Remember that contrary to DOS, UNIX uses a foreslash "/" to separate directory names.

Table 2.1   Quick UNIX Commands

Command	Description
bye	Closes a connection with a remote host. Same as quit.
cd	Changes directory. Using cd will change the current working directory to the one you specify after the cd command. To change back to a parent directory (one level above the current working directory), use cd .. but be sure to include a space between the .. and the cd. The root directory is indicated by a single "/" and does not have a higher level parent directory.
cat *<filename>*	ConCATenate. May be used similarly to DOS TYPE to display the contents of a file. Be careful not to make the mistake of trying to display a non-text (for example, graphics or program) file, or unpredictable results may ensue.

continues

Table 2.1   Continued

Command	Description
cat README.TXT	Displays the contents of README.TXT. If a file is so large that it scrolls by too fast to read, use cat in conjunction with the more command.
cp *<source> <destination>*	Copy. Creates a copy of the source file, and names it as destination. Full directory paths may be specified.
date	Returns the current system date.
ls	Short listing or "list short." The ls command is similar to the DOS dir command and will give a listing of all file and directory names in the current working directory. For a more detailed list, use ls -l to return file names with dates and sizes.
logout	Terminates a session connection with a remote host.
man *<command>*	Displays the manual page for a command, detailing proper usage. Man pages are written by computer people for computer people, so the information may not be very useful to the novice.
mkdir *<directoryname>*	Creates (makes) a directory.
mv *<source> <destination>*	Moves file from source to destination. Similar to cp, but the source file no longer exists after moving it to the destination.

Command	Description
more	Halts the output of a command, such as CAT, at the bottom of the screen, displays - MORE - and waits for the user to press any key to continue.
pwd	Prints working directory. Returns the current working directory path that the user is in.
whereis *<filename>*	Returns a directory path to the file <filename>.
who	Displays a list of users currently logged in to a local network.

Three special key sequences are used to send UNIX instructions, by holding down the Control (Ctrl) key and pressing the appropriate letter. They are:

Ctrl+C	Cancels a process
Ctrl+D	Terminates input
Ctrl+Z	Suspends a process

Success at navigating a UNIX system improves with experience, so be patient, and type carefully!

Learning Netiquette

"Netiquette" is a neologism derived from "Net," a short form for "Internet" and "etiquette." As you have seen, a wealth of information exists in cyberspace; however, the Internet is also about people and interacting with them. As with all human interaction, courtesy should be your guide in all virtual behaviors. Some rules have developed to help us know how to act in certain situations. Two of my colleagues have provided a 12-step netiquette guide as part of their book *English Online: A Student's Guide to the Internet and World Wide Web*; the information they provide is so good I thought I would pass some of it on to you here.

Protect Your Privacy and That of Others

Not all Internet activities are secure. For example, when you send information through Netscape, a pop-up screen often appears that informs you that the information you are sending can be intercepted by a third party. Moreover, your e-mail can be read by system administrators and, in some states, is even considered the property of the school or university. To protect yourself, make sure to choose a password that combines both numbers and characters. Do not choose a password that spells the name of any of your family members or reflects your birthdate. These kinds of passwords are the first that computer hackers will try.

Learn and Follow the Acceptable Use Policy

Often, school systems will devise a set of policies that govern employees' and students' use of the Internet. These policies may limit the amount of information you can store under your computer account or rules governing recreational use of the Internet. If your school has such a policy, make yourself and your students aware of any restrictions.

Stand by Your Words

When communicating via the Internet, whether by e-mail or chat technology, you exist primarily in the words you write; what you say is who you are. Consequently, take the time to think carefully about what you want to say and try to avoid using language or terms that may be misconstrued.

End E-Mail with Your Name and Address

Not all mail programs will append your name and address information to all messages you send. Putting this information at the end of your e-mail message will make it easier for others to contact or respond to you directly.

Never Leave the Subject Heading Blank

Try to use subject headings for your messages that closely reflect the content of your message. Many people on the Internet overlook this simple courtesy and use the "reply" function of their mail program which inserts the same subject heading. It is often annoying to receive messages that purport to deal with one subject when in fact they deal with an entirely different one.

Make Sure to Credit Your Sources

Always give proper credit for anything you use or find on the Internet—even mail messages. While e-mail is not considered an official publishing forum, it is still courteous to acknowledge the source of your information. If you quote e-mail in another venue—a paper, an article, or essay, try to get permission from the writer you are quoting.

Stay Cool When Flamed

Since all Internet interaction is accomplished through writing, misunderstandings are bound to arise. If someone misinterprets your message and responds hostilely (flaming), try to remain cool and respond with wit and good humor.

Helping Students Explore the Internet

The following assignments are designed to help your students get started using the Internet for research.

Exploration Assignment 2.1:
Exploring Gopherspace

Subject: All

Grade-level: 4-12

Description: Students explore the resources available to them for research by browsing gopherspace at the University of Minnesota.

Objective: To help students discover how to operate a gopher client, and to use it to find information in preparation for more advanced searching techniques.

Preparation: Ensure that your students have access to a telnet or gopher client. Write the location, **consultant.micro.umn.edu (134.84.132.4)**, on the blackboard or somewhere the students can see it easily.

Procedure:

1. After logging into the system, direct the students to gopherspace and encourage them to browse and take notes on the resources that they encounter.

2. Students should share the results of their exploration with classmates, either orally or in a short report.

Tip for Success With younger students, you may want to assign a topic that you've investigated in advance to ensure they don't become overwhelmed with all the information they retrieve from a search.

Exploration Assignment 2.2:
Searching with Veronica

Subject: All

Grade-level: 4-12

Description: Students discover how to conduct a search of gopherspace using Veronica as a tool.

Objective: To provide students with the basic skills necessary to perform keyword search operations in preparation for more advanced search techniques.

Preparation: Ensure that your students have access to a gopher client, and the location, **consultant.micro.umn.edu (134.84.132.4)**.

Procedure:

1. After logging into the system, direct the students to the item "Search Gopherspace Using Veronica."

2. Direct students to perform a simple search, one using "and," one using "or," and one using "not" operations.

3. Have students share their results with other group members or with the whole class.

Tip for Success With younger students, you may want to assign a topic that you've investigated in advance to ensure they don't become overwhelmed with all the information they retrieve from a search.

Exploration Assignment 2.3:
Archie and FTP

Subject: All

Grade-level: 4-12

Description: Students employ archie to search for a file location, then perform the commands necessary to transfer it using ftp.

Objective: To help students discover how to operate an archie client and to use it to find information; to help students learn to transfer files using ftp to obtain information used in research.

Preparation: Ensure that your students have access to an archie and ftp client, and an archie location such as **archie.rutgers.edu**.

Procedure:

1. After logging into the system, direct the students to use archie and search for a file of interest. Have them record the location of the file that they desire.

2. Demonstrate the use of ftp to connect anonymously to a site. Once connected, indicate the commands necessary to navigate directories to the location of the file of interest.

3. Stress the use of the BIN command to ensure proper file transfer. Have the students acquire a file, and show them how to decompress it if necessary.

Tip for Success With younger students, you may want to assign a topic that you've investigated in advance to ensure they don't become overwhelmed with all the information they retrieve from a search.

A Look Both Ways

This chapter has looked at ways to find information on the Internet. We've seen the wealth of material that is out there in gopherspace and on the Internet. For those interested in exploring the World Wide Web, Chapter 8 will get you started. The following chapter will begin looking at how to use e-mail technology in your classroom.

Communicating Faster, Cheaper, and Farther

Once upon a time in a kingdom long ago and far away, people wrote letters to one another. Long, detailed accounts of daily lives, ideas, and reflections. Indeed, people spent the better part of a morning writing letters—setting up appointments, turning down invitations, discussing the morning paper, or the latest play or serialized novel. Often, these letters took the form of "conversations" and extended over several weeks or months—not surprising, given the time it took for letters to reach their destinations. Then a blight came upon the kingdom—the telephone—and letter writing became obsolete. A complication of this new black plague led to the decline of the U.S. Postal Service, thus ensuring the demise of the letter.

The development of the Internet, however, has breathed new life into this near-extinct activity, merging the speed of the telephone with the capability for written, extended discourse. E-mail, or electronic mail, provides an entirely new venue for communication—fast, economical, and global. Still in its infancy, e-mail is primarily used for short, businesslike communications. However, that usage says far more about our society than about the medium; nothing about e-mail precludes its use as a medium for more extended discourses. Indeed, as we become more familiar with its use, as it becomes more and more a part of our everyday lives, hope exists that we may once again find epistolary interactions even more fulfilling than they were once upon a time. But such satisfaction with letter writing will take time and, most important, education.

TECH TALK **Snail mail:**
Mail sent via the postal service; a snail of another gender; antonym of "e-mail."

E-Mail Extends the Classroom

Until recently, the classroom interactions of most students were limited to face-to-face and written communication with the teacher and other class or school members. As we know, such interactions are important to the learning process. Yet all too often, students in a given class hail from a fairly homogeneous population. In my own classes, for example, approximately 98 percent of the students come from very similar socioeconomic backgrounds and share comparable religious and ethical beliefs.

While this state of affairs poses little problem in terms of teaching content knowledge, it is extremely debilitating when the goal is to teach argumentation or persuasion or critical thinking. Students have little impetus to defend a position that virtually all their peers share. Moreover, the tendency of a group to reinforce shared beliefs and opinions and reject difference is compounded in most homogeneous classroom environments. Having students create "dissenting audiences" with whom to communicate is often an exercise in futility. They simply don't know how to do that, having never really interacted with others of widely divergent belief systems. You can't "make up" an audience about which you have absolutely no knowledge.

Even in culturally diverse classrooms, the problem with confronting difference remains. Many students of "other" backgrounds are desperately seeking to become "Americans," to merge with and adopt the dominant ideological climate.

E-mail, however, goes far toward alleviating this lack of experience with dealing with difference. Students can communicate with others from across the nation, from around the world. "Real" questions about identity, value systems, beliefs—*genuine differences*—arise and must be confronted in a tangible way.

For example, last year my students had the opportunity to interact via e-mail with a class of Japanese students. The Japanese students wrote letters of introduction to my class. Every letter followed exactly the same format, provided exactly the same information, including the student's blood type. My students were absolutely shocked and at a complete loss about what to do or how to respond.

We discussed the issue in class, developing a context that would render the uniformity of the letters understandable. We also discussed the importance of blood type in the context of the Japanese concept of self-identity. My students then responded with letters of introduction of their own that included their astrological signs. See E-Mail Project 3.2, Reach Out and Write Someone, for a full description of this activity.

 **e-pals:**
The 20th-century equivalent of pen pals.

Increasing Student-Teacher Contact

E-mail can be used for a variety of classroom purposes. Students can use e-mail to ask you questions as they work in the library or, possibly, at home. You could respond to their questions that same day or include an answer in your preparation for the next day's class. Conversely, you can contact students readily if the need arises. If you have a question about a student's homework response, for example, you might write to that student requesting elaboration. The student can then respond to you via e-mail.

The greatest benefit of inviting your students to communicate with you via e-mail is that it gives them a sense of greater power over their learning. An additional benefit is that all these exchanges take place through writing. And as we know, students need all the practice they can get communicating through writing. You can make general class announcements via e-mail as well. Finally, with access to e-mail, students never again have an excuse to turn in late work. If they can't finish an assignment before class, I allow them to e-mail it to me by the end of the day.

I remember one exchange I had with a student who was working on a project one evening in the school's computer lab while I was at home. I received an "urgent" e-mail from her the night before a project was due requesting help with integrating graphics into her report. "It just won't work," she screamed via e-mail. (Screaming in e-mail is accomplished by typing your message in all capital letters.) I responded immediately, telling her to calm down, we'd get through it.

I told her to write and explain what she was trying to do and *exactly* what steps she was taking. I then responded with instructions of my own. Over the next half hour we exchanged e-mail until she had succeeded. The exchange required her to communicate her process accurately and completely, to decode my instructions, and to examine how that differed from what she was doing. She learned far more than simply how to put a graphic into her text file.

> **Note** Avoid drowning in e-mail. Once students know they can contact you outside of class, their tendency is to do so. Often! Be careful that you don't end up constantly responding to student requests.

Increasing Student-Student Contact

Students rarely get to interact with one another in intellectual ways outside the classroom. E-mail can genuinely help students become more independent and "authoritative" when used in a mentoring program. In this type of situation, students from one class serve as mentors for younger students from another class. The mentoring can take many forms, from helping students master course content to helping students adjust to new grade levels.

Using E-Mail in the Writing Process

Writing is a process, not just the creation of a final product. Although I don't absolutely require multiple drafts on a paper assignment, I invite (actually strongly urge) my students to send me copies of their work in progress for my review and comments.

For a variety of reasons, students seem less threatened when they submit their work electronically. Something about the formality and finality of cold, hard print seems to make students reticent about sharing their work. The computer screen makes writing seem transient; the words that appear on the screen disappear when you close the file or send the e-mail message. This seeming ephemerality puts students more at ease about their writing.

Consequently, many of my students do share their ongoing work with me more readily and consistently. I generally respond to these drafts the same day I receive them. Again, rapid response is the key. Students see then that writing and drafting are actually parts of an ongoing conversation, not something they do solely in isolation.

I'm one of those rare birds who actually prefers to comment on these drafts right on the screen. Many of my colleagues must print out student work in order to respond effectively.

When responding to student writing electronically, I place my comments in a paragraph below their text. I never write directly in their text. I also make sure to put my comments in another color or in capital letters so they are easily differentiated from the student's text.

Again, my comments to their drafts are limited to *responses*, not critiques. I don't point out spelling or mechanical errors; I don't "correct" their writing in any way. I constrain my activity to issues of content, raising questions to push their thinking, pointing out areas that I don't understand. I try to convey to the student the sense that we're conversing about the subject; I act as a peer instead of a judge.

Students benefit greatly from this exchange as does the quality of their work. Instead of feeling threatened by being judged at every point in their learning, they become more relaxed, more apt to take risks and stretch farther.

Tip for Success You might consider saving these ongoing drafts. You can then review them and use them to help the students better understand the revision process.

Electronic Peer Review

E-mail can also be used to share drafts of work in progress with other students. Students can e-mail one another copies of their ongoing drafts for peer review and comment. I've long been a proponent of peer review as part of my teaching of the writing process. I've also struggled the whole time with balancing time for peer review with time for the necessary classroom instruction. Often, I've had to play a precarious juggling act throughout the semester.

With e-mail, the problems have been mitigated to a large degree. My students send copies of the drafts to other members of their working groups and get feedback—outside of class. I provide handouts on the peer review process as well as specific questions for them to address early in the semester via e-mail. To ensure that students are keeping up with this aspect of course requirements, I ask them to send a copy of their responses to other students' work to me. (See E-Mail Project 3.4: Electronic Peer Review.)

Collaborative Writing Projects

E-mail is also ideally suited to collaborative writing projects. Collaborative writing can be one of the most fulfilling academic and human endeavors—or it can be a nightmare. Complaints about unequal work division and complaints about the inability to meet with other group members are greatly alleviated by e-mail.

I recently had the chance to write collaboratively with five of my colleagues (whom I had never met) from around the world. It was an experience that I will always cherish; in fact, in many ways, I never want to write alone again. I try to offer my students a similar experience every semester.

The process strongly resembles traditional collaborative writing projects. Students can e-mail drafts of their work among their group members for continued drafting and revision. Each group member makes his or her contribution and e-mails copies of the current draft to all other group members. Make sure you tell students to save a copy of all of his or her e-mail messages. (See E-Mail Project 3.3: Let's Write Together.)

Tip for Success Make sure students understand that only one person at a time works on the current draft. Otherwise, students will become confused as to which draft is the most current, or worse yet, all will start writing at the same time.

E-Mail Named #1 Factor in Rain Forest Preservation

With the advent of electronic mail, paper use and duplicating costs are potentially radically diminished. Think of all the time you can save not having to make all those copies! E-mail can also cut down on the amount of paper students need to generate. I ask my students to submit their work to me electronically, not in hard copy.

I no longer have to tote home mounds of paper or worry about my dogs chewing up their homework. We are on our way to becoming a paperless society. Remember, though, not to duplicate your efforts; don't send (or request) both electronic and print-based communications.

The Electronic Journal

One of the most fruitful uses of e-mail in classes is its use in student electronic journals—e-journals. We're all familiar with journal assignments and the frustration we often feel when students write solely for themselves or for us.

E-mail allows for a more public forum for student journal writing. Students can share their responses to journal topics via e-mail to you, to one another, or via a class listserv. (See Chapter 4 for an extended discussion of listservs, and Listserv Project 4.1: Collaborative Journaling, for a description of the shared electronic journal.)

Discovery surely happens through writing, but it happens more frequently and easily when ideas are shared, altered, and reshaped through feedback.

In this activity, students e-mail you a weekly diary or journal entry; you, in turn, respond to the entries by e-mail.

The greatest advantage of this method of journaling is that students needn't wait a week or longer before getting your response. We all know what happens when we receive a stack of student writing; it's impossible to get through them all in a short period of time.

Research has borne out the human truth that we become more motivated with a rapid response to our actions and less motivated when we have to wait. E-mail goes far toward reducing the response time to student work. The most important thing to remember, however, is to stagger the due dates for the journal. Divide your class into five groups and designate a different day of the week for their journal due dates. You'll find that responding to five student journal entries a day is much easier than responding to 25 at a time. (See E-mail Project 3.1: The Electronic Diary for a detailed discussion of this activity.)

Getting Familiar with E-Mail

Numerous programs have been written to simplify the e-mail process. In the earliest days, UNIX mail was the only post office in town. Shortly thereafter, Pine became popular with users still working within a UNIX environment. With the advent of graphical user environments, such as the Macintosh operating system and Windows, more and more programs are emerging. The most popular of these are MS Mail, Eudora, and Pegasus Mail. Netscape, the fastest growing World Wide Web browser, has even added a mail component to its array of built-in features. However, bear a couple caveats in mind when thinking about using e-mail with your students:

■ First and foremost, bear in mind that not all people use the same e-mail program. Most differences among the programs are superficial; however, certain programs encode the mail differently, rendering it unreadable in another mail program.

■ Moreover, some programs are more limited than others in their ability to decode messages written in a word-processing format. Eudora, for example, is more limited than Pegasus in the types of files it can send and read. Hence, the best plan is to start out by having students type their text directly into the mail message. As students become more familiar with e-mail, you can encourage them to write longer, more extended discourses in a word processor and have them attach those files in an e-mail message.

E-Mail Basics

Everyone connected to the Internet has his or her own unique electronic address. Realizing that the U.S. Postal Service ran into serious trouble with their nomenclature system, the designers of the electronic mail system decided to introduce some order into naming conventions. Electronic addressing isn't flawless, but the system is still in its infancy.

First, of course, comes your name, which can take many forms depending on your school's naming conventions. Your e-name could be your first initial and last name, it could be in the form of your firstname.lastname, or it could be a series of letters and numbers. Some schools even allow you to make up your own e-name, but most follow the developing Internet standard of firstname.lastname. My e-name, for example, is jane.lasarenko, although our computer system will also recognize jlasarenko and jane.

After your name comes the "at" sign (@). Then comes the name of your school, organization, company, or Internet service provider, followed by a single dot (.). All e-mail address sections are separated by a dot.

Note E-mail addresses are typed as one long string; never insert any spaces between the parts.

The rest of the e-mail address tells the electronic postmaster where your computer mailbox is located. E-mail addresses are sorted into general areas based on our societal divisions. The system is rather feudal (we obviously haven't come that far), but it's a start. Addresses are sorted as follows:

Address	Designation
.k12	School districts
.edu	Colleges and universities
.org	(Generally) nonprofit organizations
.com	Commercial organizations
.gov	Government entities
.mil	Military entities

Thus, my address, **jlasarenko@wtmail.wtamu.edu** tells the Internet that my mailbox is located on a machine called "wtmail," which is located at the educational institution "wtamu."

Often, you'll see a two-letter appendage after the organization identifier. These two-letter codes indicate countries. For example, if I happened to teach at a school in the United Kingdom, my address would read **jlasarenko@wtmail.wtamu.edu.uk**. Other common country codes you might come across are **jp** for Japan and **ca** for Canada.

Getting Started with E-Mail

The following instructions are designed to get you started using the e-mail capability of the Netscape browser, rather than a specific mail program. Most everyone connected to the Internet is familiar with Netscape; its mail features resemble those of most e-mail programs. Students, too, are probably best served by learning to use Netscape's e-mail because they won't always have access to a stand-alone e-mail package.

Accessing Netscape's E-Mail

Netscape's mail function can be accessed in one of two ways: either through the File menu at the top of the screen (to send mail), as shown in Figure 3.1, or by clicking the little envelope icon on the bottom right of the screen (to get mail), as shown in Figure 3.2.

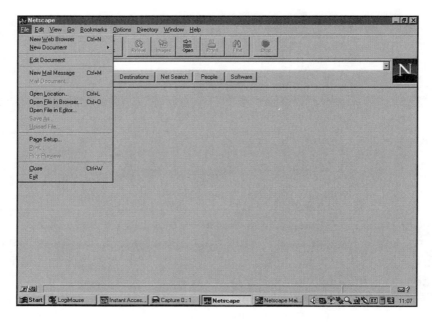

Fig. 3.1 To locate Netscape mail, choose File, New Mail from the menu.

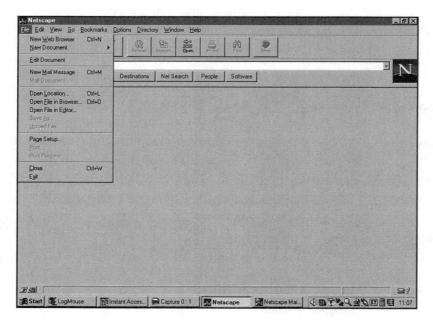

Fig. 3.2 To get your mail in Netscape, click the Get Mail icon.

Sending Mail in Netscape

Sending mail in Netscape is very easy. When you choose File, New Mail Message, the screen shown in Figure 3.3 comes up.

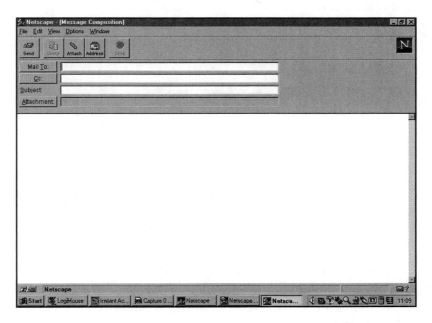

Fig. 3.3 You can send your mail via the Compose Mail Message Editor.

Fill in the information requested on each line and click the Send button on the toolbar.

Retrieving Mail in Netscape

Getting your mail in Netscape is as easy as clicking the envelope icon at the bottom of the Netscape screen. (The same icon also appears at the bottom of the New Mail Message screen.) Clicking the envelope icon brings up the screen shown in Figure 3.4.

As you can see, the Mail screen is divided into three main areas. In the left section is a list of your folders with information about how many messages are currently in each. As you highlight a folder, the individual messages in that folder appear in the right section. For example, the "Inbox" folder in

Figure 3.4 is holding one message (listed as unread). That message is from "Mozilla," and its subject is "Welcome," as identified in the right folder. The example also shows that five messages are waiting in the Sent folder. If we highlighted that folder, its five messages would be listed in the right section.

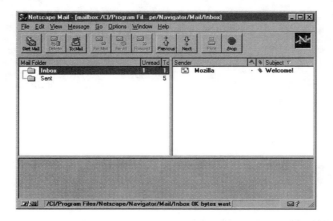

Fig. 3.4   Get your mail in Netscape from the main Mail screen.

When you highlight a message listed in the right section, the text of the message appears in the lower portion of the screen.

> **TECH TALK   Folder:**
> A short form of "file folder;" a subdirectory for storing documents.

> **Tip for Success** If you prefer a larger viewing area for your messages, you can adjust the size by placing your cursor over the divider. Your cursor will then change to a small bar with an arrow above and below it. Press and hold down the left mouse button and move the border to the location you prefer.

Saving E-Mail in File Folders

As you noticed in Figure 3.4, two folders are listed on the left side of the screen: Inbox and Sent. Those folders, along with the Trash folder are the basic ones that come with Netscape's mail program. You can add as many folders as you like. I have some 20 working mail folders currently and, knowing me, I'll be adding to those shortly. In some mail programs, you can even create folders within folders.

To create a new mail folder, choose File, New Folder. A dialog box appears prompting you for the name of the new folder (see Figure 3.5). Type the name you desire and click OK. Your new folder will appear on the screen.

Fig. 3.5 Use the New Folder screen to add a new file folder.

Moving Messages to Mail Folders

Well, you've got the folder created; now you need to sort your mail into the appropriate folders. To do so, you simply highlight the mail message you want to move (see Figure 3.6).

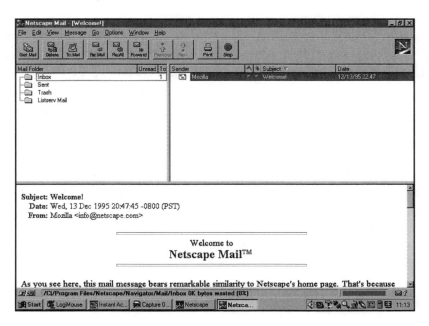

Fig. 3.6 A mail message is highlighted and ready to be moved to another folder.

Hold down the left mouse button and drag the message to the New Folder icon on the left side. Release the mouse button, and your message has been moved, as shown in Figure 3.7.

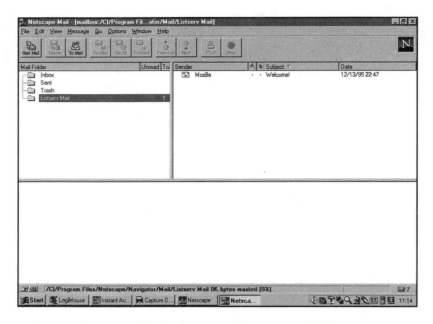

Fig. 3.7 The mail message has been moved to a new folder.

Sending Attachments with Your Message

Often, you'll want to send an attachment with your e-mail messages. These attachments can be anything from a page you've found on the World Wide Web to comments on a student draft or a draft of your own to a colleague for review. Having to retype that draft into the body of an e-mail message would be a nightmare. Fortunately, you can attach the file to your message. Attaching files to your e-mail messages is as easy as clicking the Attach button in the Send New Message screen, as shown in Figure 3.8.

The Attach button is the third from the left. When you click Attach, the dialog box shown in Figure 3.9 appears.

Fig. 3.8 Sending an attachment in Netscape begins by clicking the Attach button.

Fig. 3.9 Use the Attachments dialog box to attach a file to an e-mail message.

You can use the Attach Location URL button to mail a copy of the current Web page. To attach a file, click the Attach File button. When you click the Attach File button, a screen asks you to find and click the file you want to attach (see Figure 3.10).

Fig. 3.10   Use the Enter File to Attach screen to attach a file to your e-mail message.

Navigate and click the file you want to attach and click Open or OK depending on your software. The name of the file you selected should now appear in the Attachments screen, as shown in Figure 3.11.

Fig. 3.11   The name of your attached file is listed in this dialog box.

That's all there is to it! Now just click the Send button to send your message along with the attached file.

Reading a Message that Has an Attachment

In Netscape, messages that have attachments appear as shown in Figure 3.12.

Note that Part 1.2 is highlighted. When you click the icon, the screen shown in Figure 3.13 appears, prompting you to save the file in the location of your choice.

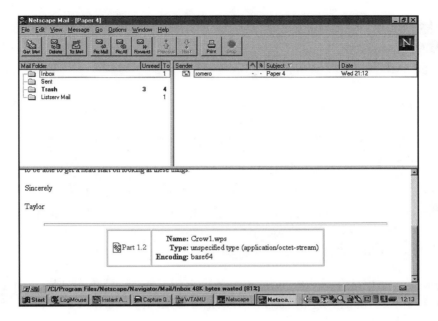

Fig. 3.12 This e-mail has an attachment, indicated by the icon included with the message.

Fig. 3.13 You must save the attached file to disk before you can open it.

You can now open your attachment in your favorite word processor to read it.

Introducing Students to E-Mail

The following assignments are designed to break down the basic skills involved in using e-mail, focusing on the kinds of activities students will use the most and need for the larger projects described later in this chapter and the next.

Assignment 3.1: Learning to Send an E-Mail Message

Subject: All

Grade level: All

Objective: To provide students the skills necessary for sending and reading e-mail messages.

Description: Put your students into pairs for this activity. (If you have an odd number of students, you should pair with the extra student.) Each student should write a letter of introduction or a letter describing his or her favorite hobby to the other member of the pair.

Preparation: Make sure that each student has a valid e-mail address. There's nothing more frustrating to students than to write a letter that can't be sent.

Procedure:

1. Have one student open the Compose New Message screen in Netscape and enter the e-mail address of the pair member. Depending on the grade level of your students, you may have to make sure they have all typed the information correctly.

2. Have each student compose a short letter and send it to the other student. Wait about five minutes.

3. Have the second student open the New Mail Messages screen and read the new letter.

4. Have the second student respond by writing a new mail message (not by using the reply function) to the original letter writer.

Assignment 3.2: Learning to Attach and Extract Files

Subject: All

Grade level: All

Objective: To help students learn to attach files to their e-mail files and to read files that have attachments.

Description: Have students exchange recent pictures of themselves with an e-pal. This assignment works well with E-Mail Project 3.2: Reach Out and Write Someone.

Preparation: Ask students to bring in a recent picture. Scan the pictures into the computer and save them in .JPG or .GIF format, the two formats Netscape is able to display. (See Chapter 8 for more detail about pictures in Netscape.)

Procedure:

1. Have each student open the file with his or her picture in Netscape to see how the picture came out by choosing File, Open File in Browser.

2. Have students compose an e-mail message to their e-pals or another class member.

3. Have the students attach their picture file to the message.

4. Have the students send the message.

Computer Pictures Are Worth a Thousand Words

Kids love to see their pictures on the computer—well, don't we all? This assignment acts as a real motivator for students to learn to use the computer. If *you* are unsure how to save pictures in computer format, ask an art teacher or someone on the computer staff for help.

E-Mail Projects

These projects will get your students going with e-mail before advancing to more sophisticated e-mail projects involving listservs (see Chapter 4).

E-Mail Project 3.1: The Electronic Diary

Subject: All

Grade level: 3-12

Description: Electronic diaries (or journals) resemble their print counterparts and are used in much the same way. The primary difference, of course, is that these diaries are submitted—and responded to—electronically. One of the great advantages of doing journaling activities electronically is that you can easily maintain a record of student entries with your responses in a folder, thereby tracking student progress more easily and closely.

Objective: To provide students the opportunity to demonstrate metacritical thinking skills in their writing activities.

Procedure:

1. Explain your particular journaling demands to the students. For this kind of activity, I generally ask students to reflect on their learning in class or from the text book, reserving more topic-oriented discussions for a class listserv (see Network Project 5.1: The Collaborative Class Journal).

2. Divide your class into five groups of 5 to10 students depending on the overall class size.

3. Announce journal due dates for each of the five groups—for example, group 1 is due Monday; group 2, Tuesday; and so forth. Stagger the due dates so that you will be able to respond to journals within 24 hours.

4. Have students e-mail you their journal entries on their due dates.

5. Respond to student journals as quickly as possible.

Assessment: Regardless of subject content, I use these journals to push students to reflect on their learning and learning processes. I never grade their writing *per se,* nor do I mark mechanical errors. I let students know that these communications are private—just between us. They are to use the space to express difficulties, successes, questions, and ideas about their performance or the subject matter. For older students, I require more extensive and formal entries (and less frequent), based upon the five dimensions of learning: confidence, use of prior and emerging experience, content knowledge, skill knowledge, and reflection.

E-Mail Project 3.2: Reach Out and Write Someone

Subject: All

Grade level: All

Description: This project stems from the traditional pen-pal projects of earlier years. Students communicate with someone from another school or geographic region about topics they are studying.

Objective: To improve students' writing skills, to extend their understanding of a topic, and to broaden their horizons and improve human relations skills.

Preparation: Contact another teacher of a similar grade level and subject matter. Be sure you both agree on when to start the project (again rapid response is a key motivator) and on the general aims of the project. Ascertain, also, whether you both plan this to be an in-class or out-of-class activity, as well as how you plan to monitor student activity. For example, you might plan to have students send you a copy of the messages they send to their e-pals, at least in the beginning stages.

Procedure:

1. Provide students with the name and e-mail address of their e-pal.

2. Have students write a short e-mail letter of introduction to their e-pal and send it.

3. Allow time the next day to have students access their e-mail to read the response.

4. Specify a topic for their communications. (I generally assign topics once a week.)

5. Have students report in class on the responses of their e-pals when appropriate.

Assessment: Students, particularly younger ones, love this project. There's nothing more motivating than forming a relationship with someone who lives in a different part of the country—or of the world. Again, I never grade students on this activity, neither on quantity nor quality. The point of the project is to get students involved with the subject matter and to verbalize their ideas.

Variations: Along with letters, students can send pictures of themselves, their home town, and their favorite things. Older students can exchange research information and drafts of papers.

Tip for Success The more preparation you and the other teacher make regarding the parameters of this activity, the more successful it generally is, particularly with younger students. Young students are often shy about communicating with others they don't know. Make sure everyone involved understands what they are supposed to write, to whom, and the time period in which to respond to another's letter.

E-Mail Project 3.3: Let's Write Together
Subject: All

Grade level: All

Description: This project asks students to work on an extended piece of writing together. Students learn a great deal about the writing process and how to blend several voices into a community voice.

Objectives: To provide students the opportunity to experience the joy of writing collaboratively; to help students improve writing skills; to help students improve interpersonal and team skills.

Procedure:

1. Divide students into groups of five. (Research shows that groups of five are generally the most successful.)

2. Provide handouts on the assignment.

3. Have students adopt specific initial roles: drafter, reviser 1, reviser 2, editor, and so on.

4. The student drafter should circulate an initial draft of the paper to all group members via e-mail. However, only reviser 1 should actually work on the draft.

5. Reviser 1 should then circulate the revision (or continuation) to all other group members.

6. All members of the group should comment on this initial draft via e-mail with all other group members.

7. Reviser 2 should collect all comments and make appropriate revisions and extensions to the paper. Copies of the new draft should be circulated to all group members.

8. Again, all members of the group should comment on this second draft via e-mail.

9. Reviser 3 should then make all appropriate revisions and extensions to the paper.

10. Repeat steps 6-9 until all the group members are satisfied with the product or until the due date.

11. Have students tell you about their experience of the project in an e-mail letter or a journal entry.

Assessment: As in all collaborative writing situations, much depends on the individual group member's skills going into the project. To the extent possible, try to make the groups as diverse as possible in terms of skills, gender, personality type, and background. When the project is finished, ask students to reflect on their experience, addressing such issues as how it differed from other writing experiences and how they felt about their group members at various points in the process. If problems arose, how were they handled by those involved?

Variations: This project need not be a traditional research paper. Students can work collaboratively on writing stories or poems, on designing sets for a play, on descriptive pieces, or whatever is appropriate for your subject matter.

E-Mail Project 3.4: Electronic Peer Review
Subject: All

Grade level: 4-12

Description: Ask students to comment on one another's work via e-mail.

Objective: To improve student understanding of the writing process; to provide students the opportunity to share their work with their peers.

Preparation: Provide students with handouts detailing the kind of review you want them to perform.

Procedure:

1. Have students e-mail a copy of their work to a classmate.
2. The classmate should address the issues you specified in your review requirements and e-mail their comments back to the writer with a copy to you (if you desire).

Assessment: I find that electronic peer review works far better than the traditional, in-class reviews. Students are usually more willing to be honest in their assessments when the writer is not present. Again, peer review can take up valuable class time; using e-mail for peer review frees up that time.

Tip for Success Make your review requirements as specific (and limited) as possible. Electronic peer review needn't be a one-shot deal. Students could review issues of content one time and issues of organization another.

Contacting Others to Connect With

The best way to find other teachers to connect with and form e-pal projects is to join one of the many academic listservs pertinent to your subject (see Appendix B and Chapter 4 for a list of possible listservs and information about subscribing). If you want to find an international e-pal connection, try subscribing to the International E-Mail Classroom Connections (IECC) list (see Chapter 4).

Extending Your Repertoire

Mascolini, Marcia. "Getting Students Started with E-Mail." *Business Communication Quarterly* 58.3 (Sept. 1995): 38-40.

Miller, Elizabeth B. *The Internet Resource Directory for K-12 Teachers and Librarians*. 1995/96 Edition. Englewood, CO: Libraries Unlimited, Inc. 1996.

Moore, G. Robert. "Computer to Computer: Mentoring Possibilities." *Educational Leadership* 49.3 (Nov. 1991): 40.

NECC '95. "Emerging Technologies, Lifelong Learning."

Partridge, Susan. "The Inclusion of E-Mail in Our Teaching: A Discussion." ERIC No. ED383012. 1995.

Robb, Thomas and Tillyer, Anthea. "Electronically Yours: Cross-Cultural Communication Through E-Mail Penpals." Paper presented at the Annual Meeting of the Teachers of English to Speakers of Other Languages (Atlanta, GA, April 1993). ERIC No. ED366199.

Robinson, Mike. "Improving Science Teaching with E-Mail." *Computers in the Schools* 11.1 (1994): 95-107.

Silva, Pamela Urdal et al. "E-Mail: Real-Life Classroom Experience with Foreign Languages." *Learning and Leading with Technology* 23.5 (Feb. 1996): 10-12.

Warschauer, Mark. "E-Mail for English Teaching: Bringing the Internet and Computer Learning Networks into the Language Classroom." Alexandria, VA: TESOL, Inc. 1995.

Looking Both Ways

E-mail has a great deal of classroom potential: It serves to motivate student engagement with the subject matter, allows for greater student-teacher and student-student contact, and extends classroom interactions to include written communication as well as verbal. Yet e-mail in a single classroom is limited to one-on-one interactions for the most part. As we'll see in the next chapter, e-mail takes on a whole new dimension with listserv technology. Conversations via listserv technology connect students with a multitude of voices and perspectives simultaneously.

Continuing the Conversations

As you saw in the last chapter, e-mail is a terrific tool for communicating one-on-one in the classroom. However, sending messages to everyone in the class individually can get rather tedious. And, the Internet is a medium designed for multiple communication; after all, we do have telephones for one-on-one interaction. Consequently, giant worldwide mailing lists were created; these lists—called *listservs*—allow messages to be delivered to everyone who subscribes to the list.

TECH TALK **Listserv:**
A computer program for mail distribution; an electronic conference among subscribers.

Listservs are an excellent tool for Socratic learning strategies and demonstrating to students the social construction of knowledge in a concrete and profound way. Imagine engaging in a three-way conversation. You might go to the snack bar or lounge and join a conversation in which each participant has a different view of the subject. You talk, exchange your ideas and views, talk some more, and gradually reach somewhat of a consensus. Or, if dissent remains, you know more firmly where the disagreements lie.

Listservs extend this conversation, incorporating the voices of hundreds, sometimes thousands, of others from around the world. Over the past several years, I've become a "listserv junkie," thriving on the myriad conversations about composition and rhetoric taking place in cyberspace. So many of my best ideas about teaching and learning stem from the conversations taking place on the lists. Imagine what a learning experience listserv conversations could provide for your students and what an empowering experience for them to be able to add their voices to the mix.

Using Listservs to Create Extended Learning Communities

Perhaps the single most important benefit of listservs is their capacity to extend student learning situations far beyond the schoolhouse walls. College classes are generally 50 minutes per subject; all too often, the period ends just as some real, in-depth conversation begins. Such a disruption is extremely frustrating for me and cheats the students of any sense of closure on an important topic. Picking up the conversation the next class period often doesn't work—the momentum has been lost. Listservs provide a means to ameliorate these situations by allowing students to continue the conversation outside of class.

As we saw in the previous chapter, moreover, classrooms are often rather homogeneous places. Students often hesitate to express divergent views to those they must interact with every day. Listservs provide an ideal venue for students to express their views without feeling threatened. Real learning is more likely to happen when students must integrate diverse viewpoints about a subject to make it genuinely their own.

Just last semester, my students became involved in a heated discussion about Kate Chopin's book *The Awakening*. Many of the students were extremely angry with the protagonist for committing suicide. How dare she kill herself and leave her children motherless! Few in the class dared to raise their voices against the prevailing indignation. I, myself, was somewhat at a loss on how to proceed given the highly charged nature of the subject and the response.

To help myself—and the students—I asked them to subscribe to one of the American literature listservs and to raise the issue there. The ensuing debate extended the discussion outside the classroom, allowing us to move on to other subjects in class. Over the course of several weeks, students became heavily involved in the continuing debate over the story, learning far more than I could ever provide within the confines of an overly burdened syllabus.

Tip for Success Listservs vary in the amount and frequency of posts. I often receive over 50 messages a day from just one listserv! Explain to your students that they must check their e-mail every day and print out or save only those messages that they consider "important." Most student accounts are limited to a relatively small amount of disk space. After that space is used up, students can no longer send or receive messages.

Listservs also function to create a sense of community and bonding with all those "others" who belong to the list. And we all know, a sense of community fosters motivation, security, and learning. When I first arrived in the Texas Panhandle, I felt quite like the proverbial fish out of water, a reincarnated "Connecticut Yankee in King Arthur's Court." Although I wasn't the only one teaching freshman composition (we all take our share in that load), I certainly was the only one using computers in the classroom. I didn't have a single colleague with whom to share ideas about computers and writing.

I joined a listserv that dealt with the subject; I now have hundreds of colleagues around the world, engaged in the same research, the same classroom struggles, and the same successes. I have the resources of hundreds of fine minds at my disposal. I have a worldwide network of friends with whom to share my ideas. I have the sympathy of hundreds when I fail in a day's teaching and their support when I succeed with a student, class, or technique. If we are genuinely to succeed in creating a citizenry of lifelong learners, we must give our students the opportunity to partake of this kind of daily intellectual bread.

Using Listservs to Improve Student Writing and Communication Skills

For whatever reasons, students generally hold very negative views about writing. Most think of writing as "something you have to do in English classes," "pointless," and worse, "meaningless;" something they must endure. They reach adulthood wishing never to have to write again, failing to see its necessity in human affairs and interaction.

Part of the problem, I think, stems from the way we teach writing—in an English classroom with very few opportunities for using writing to effect genuine action and change in students' worlds. Even when we try our best to provide "real" or "authentic" writing situations for students, even when we try to specify audiences other than ourselves for their writing, the students perceive the activity as only a game, a ploy they go along with to please us. Listservs can go far toward alleviating this negativity and giving students an opportunity to use writing as a natural, fulfilling, and stimulating part of their lives.

Moreover, we all know that writing takes practice—lots of it. The more opportunities students have to write, the more fluent they become. In addition, the more students can write without fear of being judged with a grade, the less they will resist the task. Listservs don't dispel judgment; we are always judging people and ideas by the way they're expressed. The form of the judgment, however, shifts from grades to other means. Most important, however, is that the source of judgment shifts from us, the teachers, to a larger community.

Judgments About Writing

The primary means to signify a negative judgment in listservs, believe it or not, is silence. It's far better to have someone respond negatively, even vehemently to our ideas, than to ignore them. Being recognized, no matter how, is extremely important to human beings. Silence—indifference—is the ultimate form of rejection. One dose of it is generally enough to motivate students to improve their writing. Of course, you always face the risk of destroying a student's confidence. Make sure that if no one else responds to a student's post, you do.

Helping Students Become Members of Different Discourse Communities

One of the greatest problems young writers have is developing the flexibility to adapt their writing to different disciplines and situations. Every field has its own language, its own discourse conventions, its own way of establishing authority. Listservs expose students to these different conventions and languages, helping them to see how varied language use can be. In addition, listservs often enable students to practice writing in numerous fields and situations that generally don't arise in the classroom. Most important, these writing opportunities are ungraded. Students can write and write and write without the fear and anxiety associated with formal assignments. For many, the opportunity to write without grades is a liberating experience.

`TECH TALK` **Listserv posts:**
An individual message to the list (n); the act of sending a message to the list (v); the foundation upon which lists survive.

Helping Students Analyze Writing Conventions

Listserv topics are generally *archived,* which means that a permanent record of these messages is stored on the host computer.

`TECH TALK` **Threads:**
The messages posted to the list on a specific topic; the strands that make up the tapestry of the list.

Because a permanent record of the messages exists, students can get further practice analyzing different kinds of discourses. In the past, we were tied to analyzing essays and literature; now students can investigate shorter pieces of writing. Moreover, students can more readily grasp the conventional nature of all writing by confronting the differences in this "new" venue for writing.

For example, I often ask my students to analyze a listserv post, looking at the conventions the author uses for citing others, the reasons for that citation, and the effect of that citation on their understanding and response. Students can examine posts that are full of spelling and mechanical errors and discuss how those errors affect their understanding of the content and their response to the author.

Because listserv posts tend to be more informal than published essays, students seem less intimidated by them, less apt to take the author's word as "truth," and more likely to criticize. See Listserv Project 4.1, "Analyzing Listserv Posts and Reviewing Grammar," for more information about this activity.

Listservs Demonstrate the Social Construction of Knowledge in Action

We live in such a multivocal, complex world today. Our deepest held convictions have been challenged to the core. How difficult for today's youth! I feel such sympathy for them, yet excitement, too. We need to start helping them deal with diversity at a much younger age, and today's technology can help pave the way.

We are so sophisticated in these times; we know that knowledge is ever growing and ever suspect. We can't even be sure of the "facts" we've spent so many centuries discovering. Knowledge is for the most part, socially constructed and socially validated. The prevailing view is the right view, the fact. Students need to learn how to tread in these murky waters before they leave high school.

We've seen how successful cooperative work can be in the classroom; listservs extend this cooperation to a global scale. I know I would be paralyzed in my own research and the knotty problems of composition and learning theory were it not for the many other voices grappling with those same issues. My colleagues and I talk daily. Our talk satisfies like a well-made stew: We introduce a few topics spiced with our differing flavors; then we leave them to simmer. We test the stew through sporadic revisits and adjust the seasonings. Eventually, we come to a few realizations, a few "truths" that nourish our classrooms and help us discover the need for new spices.

Students can become far more literate about the ways in which authority works, can learn so much about how knowledge is constructed and by whom, when engaged in learning with others. See Listserv Project 4.2, "Making Meaning from Chaos," for a good project.

Using Listservs to Extend Student Research

Because listserv posts are archived, students can access them to get information on a particular topic. All too often, students see research papers as being a mere exercise designed by teachers to torture students. The largest problem by far with the papers I see is the lack of any significance or point to them. Listserv archives can genuinely help students grasp a context for their writing. After they go to the library, for example, or search the World Wide Web, they can investigate the archives of a list related to their topic to identify the debates that are current in that field.

Helping students to see that their writing is—or can be—part of an ongoing debate not only provides a purpose and context for their writing but also helps students look at writing itself in an entirely different light. Ways of providing students with this experience are detailed in Listserv Project 4.3, "Researching Listserv Archives." See "Accessing Listserv Archives" later in this chapter for information about how to access the archives.

A Listserv by Any Other Name

Listservs parade by a number of names:

- Listserv
- Listproc
- Majordomo
- Maiser

Don't let all these pseudonyms fool you; they're all aliases for the same computer postmistress. Even the World Wide Web has its equivalent—a program called Hypermail (or HyperNews for USENET groups; see the "Taking Advantage of USENET Newsgroups" section later in this chapter for more information). These pseudonyms are important only insofar as the type of listserv program on a machine determines how you subscribe to the list.

Subscribing to a Listserv

Three addresses are generally associated with all listservs: the subscription address, the list address, and the moderator's address. These addresses correspond to the address you write to subscribe to the list, the address you write to send a message to the list itself, and the address of the person in charge of the list.

Subscribing to a listserv is really quite simple—just write a message to the computer mail program, the subscription address, as shown in Figure 4.1.

- Type the subscription address in the To field of your mail message.

- Leave the Subject field empty; do not type in a subject.

- In the Message field, type:

    `Subscribe <listname> <yourfirstname> <yourlastname>`

Be sure to substitute the real name of the list and your real first and last names in place of the angle brackets.

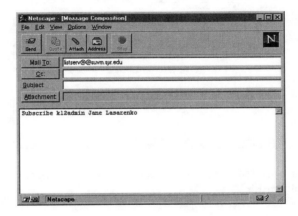

Fig. 4.1   This mail message shows how to subscribe to the k12admin listserv.

Note Some listserv programs such as Majordomo require that you send your e-mail address instead of your name when subscribing. If your subscription request doesn't work or if you get a mail message back indicating that the program doesn't understand your request, resend it with your e-mail address instead of your name.

You should receive a welcome message back if your subscription request was successfully processed. Be sure to save that welcome message; it contains valuable information about the list as well as information about how to unsubscribe.

Thereafter, you should send all messages to the *list address* (see Figure 4.2). You will write to the subscription address only one more time—when you unsubscribe from the list. Unsubscribing from the list follows the same process as subscribing; the only difference is that in the Message field, you type

```
unsubscribe <listname><yourfirstname><yourlastname>
```

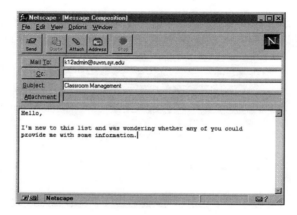

Fig 4.2 Sending a message to a list is the way you can participate in a discussion on a particular topic.

The main difference between the subscription address and the list address is that when writing to the list, you use the name of the list; when subscribing, you use the name of the listserv program in the To field.

Setting Listserv Mail Options

You may want to alter the listserv default options: for example, when you leave town for a time, when activity gets heavy on certain mail lists, or when you want to restart your mail when you return from a vacation. Table 4.1 provides a list of listserv mail options; for Listproc listservs, the command is given in parentheses. Majordomo lists do not currently support these listserv commands. All the commands are sent to the list subscription address in the following format:

`listserv@host.domain`

Leave the subject field blank and type the following in the message field

`<command><listname>`

Thus, if I were to need help with the commands for the list, CW-L, I would send the following to listserv@host.domain:

`help CW-L`

Table 4.1   Listserv Mail Options

Command	*Description*
`help <listname>`	Gets an overview of the listserv commands.
`unsubscribe <listname>` (signoff)	Removes you from a list.
`review () <listname>` (recipients)	Gets a listing of everyone on the list.
`set`	Used to set mail preferences as follows:
mail	Restarts sending you the list messages; used after a set nomail command.
nomail	Stops list messages when no e-mail will be available to you for a while.

continues

Table 4.1   Continued

Command	*Description*
Password <old password><new password>	Sets a new password.
address <old address><new address>	Changes your address.
conceal <yes><no>	Indicates whether your name will appear to others using a review or recipients command. (The default setting is no so you don't need to do anything if you don't mind others knowing you're on the list.)
query <listname>	Sends back a list of your current subscription options.
index <listname>	Sends an index of the list archives.

Creating a Class Listserv

Generally you'll want to ask the computer staff at your school for help in creating a separate, private list for your own class. The process isn't difficult, but unless you have access to the school server's mail program, you'll have to ask for help. The main things you'll need to provide are the name of the list and a welcome text that will be sent when someone successfully subscribes. Because you will be the list moderator—it's your list—you will have to manually enter the e-mail addresses of your students (unless you want the list to be open to the world at large).

Accessing Listserv Archives

When you want to use the list archives for research, you need to send a message to the listserv subscription address. All types of listservs use the `index` command to show archives. Thus to find out whether archives are available for a list, send the following message to **listserv@host.domain**:

```
index <listname>
```

If the specified list has no archives, the program sends you a message telling you that the archive list is "unknown." For example, if you want to see whether the ACW-L list is archived, you would send the following message to **listserv@ttacs6.ttu.edu**:

```
index Austen-L
```

The listserv program will return a message, such as the one shown in Figure 4.3, containing information about the available archives. The archive notebook in this example is created weekly under the name of the list and log date. For example, the first entry is for the archive notebook Austen-L for the first week of 1994. It was started on Sunday, January 2, 1994. The log contains 80 records (or posts), and the file is 478 lines long.

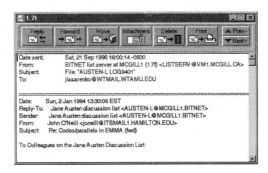

Fig. 4.3 The "Index" Command will retrieve a listing of a listserv's archives.

To receive the log, send a message to the listserv program using the `get` command. So, for example, to receive that first log, send a message to **listserv@vm1.mcgill.ca** with the following message:

```
get austen-1 log9401
```

Your request generates a file similar to the one shown in Figure 4.4.

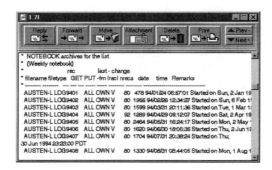

Fig. 4.4 The "get" command will send you the complete record of messages posted during the week you request.

As you can see, I have received an e-mail message that contains all the listserv posts (only the first one is visible in Figure 4.4) in log9401.

Most often, however, you will probably want to search for a specific keyword or subject, rather than for a chronological log. Let's say, for example, that you wanted all the information in the logs about Austen's book *Emma*. Listserv software allows you to search the entire database for specific subjects, authors, and keywords. Conducting listserv database searches is quite complex and requires some knowledge of programming commands. If you need more information about database searching, send a request to the listserv program with the message **help database**. For simple searches, however, the template that follows will usually get the job done.

Type the following information in the body of an e-mail message to the listserv:

```
//   JOB Echo=No
```

```
Database Search DD=Rules

//Rules DD  *

Search <keyword> IN <listname>

print

/*
```

You should receive a Database Output file containing the results of your search similar to that shown in Figure 4.5.

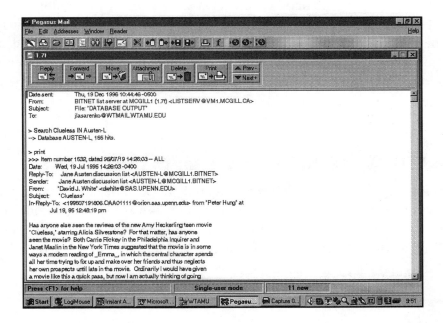

Fig. 4.5 Searching a listserv database returns only those archived messages that contain the keyword you specified.

Taking Advantage of USENET Newsgroups

USENET newsgroups are similar to listservs. The main difference between the two is that you need a special program, a news viewer, to be able to receive and read newsgroup posts. You also don't need to subscribe to them. If your school is unable to provide e-mail accounts for all students, consider using a newsgroup to implement many of the projects found later in this chapter. The main disadvantage of newsgroups is their heavy volume and that no one moderates or controls the postings. Consequently, you and your students might encounter posts that you consider "offensive" on newsgroups. I try to turn this possible liability into a teaching asset by explaining beforehand that students should be prepared to encounter ideas and language use that they might not approve of. I make a list of the ideas and words students feel are "offensive," and we agree as a class not to use those words or express those ideas. We also talk about diversity and tolerance, and discuss generally the ethics of public communication.

Teaching Students to Use Listservs

The following projects should help your students become comfortable with listservs and writing to them. Since writing to listservs involves some conventions not generally associated with letter writing, you'll need to explain these conventions. They deal with Listserv Netiquette and the use of emoticons and abbreviations in the posts.

TECH TALK **Netiquette:**
Emily Post's electronic revised edition of proper behavior online.

Emoticons:
Combinations of typographic characters used to represent emotions and states of mind. Also included are acronyms to decrease the amount of typing one needs to do (or to avoid those nasty spelling errors).

Listserv Netiquette

The courtesy, common sense, and general rules concerning language use (and abuse) that govern our daily interactions extend to our electronic activities as well. Students need to be reminded of these things for their electronic activities: "Bad" language, verbal abuse, and "flaming" are generally not tolerated on lists, and the other list members will certainly remind someone of those facts if that person's behavior gets out of hand.

> **TECH TALK** **Flaming:**
> The act of verbally abusing someone for their ideas. These actions can range from name calling to e-mail terrorism—the flooding of someone's mailbox with nonsensical messages. A "flame" can escalate to a "flame war" if both parties are so inclined.

Emoticons and Abbreviations Abound in Listserv Posts

Thousands of emoticons and abbreviations are in use in e-mail communications. Tables 4.2, 4.3, and 4.4 list some of the most popular symbols and expressions. Table 4.2 shows the most common abbreviations you might encounter on a listserv.

Table 4.2   Common Abbreviations

Abbreviation	*Description*
ack	acknowledged (usually in response to "did you get this?")
BRB	Be Right Back
BBL	Be Back Later
BTW	By The Way
CU	see you

continues

Table 4.2   Continued

Abbreviation	Description
CUL	see you later
FAQ	Frequently Asked Questions
Flame	criticize or insult
F2F	Face-to-Face
FYI	For Your Information
HND or HAND	Have a Nice Day
HTH	Hope This Helps
IMHO	In My Humble Opinion
IMO	In My Opinion
Inet	Internet
IRC	Internet Relay Chat
IRL, IPL	In Real Life, In Physical Life
JIC	Just In Case
KISS	Keep It Simple Stupid
LMK	Let Me Know
LOL	Laughing Out Loud
OBTW	Oh, By The Way
oic	oh, I see!
OTF	On The Floor (laughing)
ROTFL	Rolling On The Floor Laughing
TIA	Thanks in Advance
ttyl	Talk To You Later

Table 4.3 represents letters used to indicate emotional states or actions.

Table 4.3   Common Emotional States

Abbreviation	Description
arghh!	ultimate frustration
heheheheheheh	chuckling
ha! ha!	laughing loudly
ew...	experiencing something unpleasant
yeachhkk!	experiencing something disgusting
hhmmmm...	pondering a thought
uh-oh	worried about something bad happening
boo-hoo	crying
eeeekkkk!	scared, frightened, startled, upset
yikes!	startled, upset

Table 4.4 shows the most common emoticons on the Net. Have your students turn them sideways to see them.

Table 4.4   Common Emoticons

Emoticon	Description
:-)	smiling
:)	small smiley
:-D	laughing
;-)	winking
:-(	frowning

continues

Table 4.4 Continued

Emoticon	Description
:-<	very sad
:(	small frowney
;-(	angry
:~(	crying
:-I	thinking about something, wondering
:-|	indifferent
:-X	my lips are sealed
#-)	partied all night
[:-)	listening to headphones
:-o	surprised
:-O	big surprise

Participating in Global Discussions

These projects will stimulate your thinking about the myriad ways to use listservs in your classes. The variations are endless. After you join your own listservs, you'll get ideas from thousands of other teachers.

Listserv Project 4.1: Analyzing Listserv Posts and Reviewing Grammar

Subject: All

Grade level: 7-12

Description: This project can be altered in a variety of ways to help students understand the discourse conventions and topics of your field. Students are asked to subscribe to a subject-specific list and to write a report dealing with the form, not content, of the posts.

Objective: To help students understand the conventions by which authority is established in specific subjects and in listserv communications; to demonstrate to students how discourse communities are established and maintained.

Procedure:

1. Find a listserv in your subject area and have students subscribe.

2. Have students observe (or participate) in the listserv discussions for two or three weeks, paying attention to the following ideas:

   a. How do people seem to relate to one another? Do they seem to know one another well?

   b. What kinds of Netiquette rules are at work? How are they maintained?

   c. Who seems to be the most respected speakers on the list? How do you know that?

   How does their use of language differ from others on the list?

3. Have students write a report focusing on the preceding issues.

4. Have students share their reports with other class members.

Variations: You can use a project like this to help students review grammar and linguistic structure, or you can focus the assignment on issues of discourse communities—their formation and maintenance.

Listserv Project 4.2: Making Meaning from Chaos

Subject: All

Grade level: 9-12

Description: Listserv threads are multiple and many-voiced. Several discussions about different topics may be taking place simultaneously, and many voices are speaking about a given subject. This multiplicity is difficult for students to deal with at first, particularly in classrooms that don't have much diversity. This project is designed to help students make sense of long discussions over time and to develop critical thinking skills.

Objective: To help students develop higher-order critical thinking skills.

Procedure:

1. Have students subscribe to a listserv related to your subject.

2. Tell students to observe and save the list discussions for two to three weeks.

3. Have students write responses to the following questions:

   a. How many discussions took place over the time period?

   b. How many people participated in each discussion?

   Was there any resolution to the discussions, or did they simply stop (rather than end)?

4. Tell students to pick one of the discussions they observed to write about.

5. Have students write an informal report in which they address the following:

   a. What was the discussion topic?

   b. What was the point (or points) at issue? That is, what was the issue at the heart of the debate?

   c. Did everyone have their own views or did some people share the same view?

   d. What were the different views expressed?

   e. Did resolution or consensus take place? If so, what position did the group discussion reach? If no resolution took place, where did the discussion end?

   f. Did you agree with anyone's view(s)? Did you disagree with anyone's view(s)? What is your position on the topic?

6. Have students share their discoveries with one another.

Tip for Success You might consider having students continue the debate on their own, say on the class listserv. Students need to see that discussions take place over long periods of time and that resolution rarely occurs quickly or easily.

Listserv Project 4.3: Researching Listserv Archives

Subject: All

Grade level: 9-12

Description: A more advanced project that can be used in conjunction with Project 4.2: Making Meaning from Chaos, this activity asks students to use the material they find from listservs in a larger report. Listserv discussions are generally archived for a few years, thus providing a long-term record of "expert" opinion on a subject.

Objective: To extend student research skills from the library to the Internet; to help students learn to integrate the ideas of others into their own work.

Preparation: Gaining access to listserv archives varies from list to list. Send a request for information about accessing the archives to the list owner or to the list itself. Some lists allow keyword searches; others don't. Be sure to give students detailed information about how to search the list's archives. Otherwise, they might be totally flooded with information.

Procedure:

1. However you structure your research assignments, tell students that they will be including information obtained from listserv archives.

2. Help students practice gaining access to the list archives well in advance of their writing.

3. Have students obtain additional information and quotes from the archives for use in their assignments.

Tip for Success As with any research skill, searching archives takes practice and patience. Be prepared to provide a great deal of help to students in their research activities.

Listserv Project 4.4: Creating Geography Maps

Subject: Social Studies

Grade level: K-6

Description: This project asks students to create maps from the postcards or information they receive from other students around the state or world.

Objective: To learn geography; to form friendships with students in faraway places.

Preparation: Join one of the many e-pal listservs or make arrangements with another teacher from the state or in another country. Make sure your students have valid e-mail accounts. Draw a blank map of your state or the country you're learning about.

Procedure:

1. Have students send letters of introduction with information about your town to their e-pal.

2. Place or draw a city marker for every response location.

Variations: Older students can write letters containing only clues and descriptive information about where they live. Then recipients can deduce the city name from the clues before drawing the city marker on the map.

Listserv Project 4.5: Sending Postcard Greetings

Subject: Social Studies

Grade level: K-6

Description: This project involves kids sending postcards to other students around the world.

Objective: To help students learn about world geography; to help students enter a world community.

Preparation: Join one of the many e-pal listservs or make arrangements with another teacher from the state or in another country. If planning to send electronic postcards, make sure your students have valid e-mail accounts.

Procedure:

1. Have students purchase postcards and stamps to send to an e-pal.

2. Make sure younger students have addressed the postcards correctly.

3. Send postcards to their e-pals.

Variations: Older students can draw a postcard on the computer to send to their e-pal.

Listserv Project 4.6: Cooperative Geography

Subject: Social Studies/Geography

Grade level: 3-6

Description: This cooperative project involves students in a class dialogue about their respective geographical areas. Students ask each other questions about the topographical features of their areas.

Objective: To help students learn about rain forests, oceans, plains, mountains, and so on.

Preparation: Contact teachers in vastly disparate geographical areas who want to participate in this project. Make sure your students have valid e-mail accounts.

Procedure:

1. Have students generate a list of questions to ask the other class or classes.

2. Have students compile the responses to their questions into a short report or oral presentation.

Finding Listservs for Your Students

Many places on the Internet provide information about academic listservs; however, finding listservs specifically devoted to kids is more difficult. The following lists are excellent places to start, however. After you subscribe to your own educational lists, you'll get more suggestions and ideas. An annotated list of teaching listservs is included in Appendix B.

BR_Cafe
Subscription Address: listproc@micronet.wcu.edu
List Address: BR_Cafe@micronet.wcu.edu
Moderator's Address: Patti Johnson, **johnson@micronet.wcu.edu**

Description: A place for kids to discuss what they're reading. BR_Cafe welcomes messages of two kinds: those requesting an individual with whom to discuss a book or discussion of the book itself for the general forum discussion.

BR_Match
Subscription Address: listproc@micronet.wcu.edu
List Address: BR_Match@micronet.wcu.edu
Moderator's Address: Patti Johnson, **johnson@micronet.wcu.edu**

Description: The BR_Match list is a spin-off of the WCU BOOKREAD project. WCU BOOKREAD is a network of students and teachers of literature, communicating by computer with each other and with the authors of books they are reading in the classroom. BOOKREAD also provides a matchmaker function that helps schools connect with each other.

BR_Review
Subscription Address: listproc@micronet.wcu.edu
List Address: BR_Review@micronet.wcu.edu
Moderator's Address: Patti Johnson, **johnson@micronet.wcu.edu**

Description: For K-12 student-written book reviews. Your reviews will be read before being posted. You do not need to subscribe before posting your review, but if you want to receive all subsequent reviews, you must subscribe to BR_Review. Anyone may subscribe to BR_Review without posting a review (for instance, a student looking for a good book or a researcher looking for opinion data).

Childrens-voice

Subscription Address: listproc@schoolnet.carleton.ca
List Address: listproc@schoolnet.carleton.ca
Moderator's Address: Michael McCarthy, **mmccarthy@schoolnet. carleton. ca**

Description: This list publishes the writing of children from junior-kindergarten age to grade eight.

FISH-JUNIOR

Subscription Address: listserv@searn.sunet.se
List Address: FISH-JUNIOR@searn.sunet.se

Description: FISH-JUNIOR is a forum for marine scientists and children/high school students. The aim of this forum is to enable students to interact with scientists and learn about scientific issues (mainly related to fisheries, ecology, and related topics).

GENTALK

Subscription Address: listserv@usa.net
List Address: Gentalk@usa.net
Moderator's Address: Doug Lundberg, **lundberg@kadets.d20.co.edu**

Description: Gentalk is a list devoted to teachers and students interested in discussing issues and problems associated with genetics and biotechnology. The list provides a forum for discussing genetic problems, laboratory protocols, and current issues dealing with genetics.

IECC

Subscription Address: IECC-REQUEST@stolaf.edu
Moderator's Address: IECC@stolaf.edu
List Owner: Craig D. Rice, **cdr@stolaf.edu**

Description: The International Email Classroom Connections mailing list serves as a meeting place for teachers seeking partner classes for international and cross-cultural electronic mail exchanges. A variety of mailing lists already exist that facilitate traditional, one-on-one, pen-pal communication. This list is different in that subscribers and contributors are looking for an entire class of e-mail partners in an international or cross-cultural context. IECC-PROJECTS is for specific project discussion.

K12Pals

Subscription Address: listserv@suvm.syr.edu
List Address: K12Pals@suvm.syr.edu
Moderator's Address: Mary Beth McKee or Carol Snyder, **checkers@ericir.syr.edu**

Description: K12Pals is for elementary and secondary students who are seeking pen pals. This list is sponsored by the AskERIC Project and is open to any student or teacher involved in K-12 education. Participants may include individual or classroom pen pals. The list serves as a meeting place for those seeking pen pals; after a match is made, the parties communicate independently of the list. The requests of those seeking pen pals will be archived on the AskERIC gopher site. The actual correspondence between pen pals is private and will not be accessible to AskERIC or the list.

KIDS-ACT

Subscription Address: listserv@vm1.nodak.edu
List Address: KIDS-ACT@vm1.nodak.edu
Moderator's Address: Dan Wheeler, **dan.wheeler@uc.edu**

Description: KIDS-ACT "What can I do" project.

KIDINTRO

Subscription Address: listserv@sjuvm.stjohns.edu
List Address: KIDINTRO@sjuvm.stjohns.edu
Moderator's Address: Anne Pemberton, **apembert@vdoe386.vak12ed.edu**

Description: KIDINTRO is a list that does just that. This game for young, elementary school children involves having students interview another student in their class and send an introduction of that student to the project list. International in scope.

KIDCAFE

Subscription Address: listserv@vm1.nodak.edu
List Address: listserv@vm1.nodak.edu

Description: The purpose of KIDCAFE is to promote a global dialogue among 10- to 15-year-old kids. It tries to encourage both group discussions and individual friendships. Because of the volume of the initial KIDCAFE list, the project has been divided into five separate lists. To subscribe to each list, you need to send the following request to **listserv@vm1.nodak.edu**:

    GET KIDCAFE GUIDE

You will need to register your school before using these lists.

- KIDCAFE—INDIVIDUAL. Devoted to discussions between and among individual kids.

- KIDCAFE—SCHOOL. Devoted to discussion topics among classes rather than individuals.

- KIDCAFE—TOPICS. Open discussion.

- KIDCAFE—QUERY. Devoted to young researchers. You can send questions, surveys, and organize polls.

- KIDCAFE—COORD. Devoted to teachers participating in the project.

KIDLINK

Subscription Address: listserv@vm1.nodak.edu or **gopher:// kidlink.ccit.duq.edu**
List Address: The KIDLINK list itself is for official announcements. Each of the other lists has its own submission address.
Moderator's Address: Odd de Presno, Project Director, **KIDLINK-INFO@vm1.nodak.edu**

Description: A global dialogue for students between the ages of 10 and 15. More than 23,000 children from 62 countries have participated in a series of yearly projects beginning with KIDS-91 (through KIDS-94). The KIDLINK list itself is for distributing official information about the project; the actual dialogue takes place on several other lists run by the KIDLINK Society. Several lists are available for teachers and other adult coordinators of KIDLINK activities. Any language is acceptable on KIDLINK lists, but special lists promote communication among both students and teachers in Spanish, Portuguese, Japanese, and the Nordic languages. The headquarters of the KIDLINK Society is in Saltrod, Arendal, Norway.

KIDSNET

Subscription Address: kidsnet-request@vms.cis.pitt.edu
List Address: kidsnet@vms.cis.pitt.edu
Moderator's Address: Bob Carlitz, **carlitz@vms.cis.pitt.edu**

Description: E-conference is a global network for children and teachers in grades K-12. It is intended to provide a focus for technological development and for resolving the problems of language, standards, and so on that inevitably arise in international communications.

KIDSPHERE

Subscription Address: kidsphere-request@vms.cis.pitt.edu
List Address: Kidsphere@vms.cis.pitt.edu
Moderator's Address: Bob Carlitz, **carlitz@vms.cis.pitt.edu**

Description: Kidsphere is a list devoted to setting up an international network for the use of children and their teachers. Efforts range from getting individual classes online to planning a grand scheme to link the whole world together. The list is a good source of e-mail projects for your classes.

MATHMAGIC

Subscription Address: Contact the Moderator
List Address: Contact the Moderator
Moderator's Address: Alan A. Hodson, **alanh@laguna.epcc.edu**

Description: MathMagic is a K-12 telecommunications project developed in El Paso, Texas. It motivates students to use computer technology while increasing problem-solving strategies and communications skills. In a nutshell, MathMagic posts challenges in four categories (K-3, 4-6, 7-9, and 10-12) to trigger each registered team to pair up with another team and engage in an exchange of problem-solving dialogue. When an agreement is reached, one solution is posted for every pair. This project is for schools that are using or plan to use computers with modems. Direct Internet access is desirable (see NET-PROVIDERS file), but in some areas, a local Bulletin Board System (BBS) or Net user may have to act as a go-between. Please ask about special arrangements. OPEN lists are available to everyone and are read-only. You must register in order to participate in the discussions.

MEMORIES

Subscription Address: listserv@sjuvm.stjohns.edu
List Address: MEMORIES@sjuvm.stjohns.edu
Moderator's Address: Tom Holloway, **t.holloway@warwick.ac.uk**

Description: Another international global exchange project, MEMORIES wants people to describe what happened to them in their everyday lives during 1945. Children are encouraged to interview their grandparents and others about those times and to send their findings to the list. Those who were alive during that time are also invited to participate. Students can exchange letters with people who lived during the war years. You can find more information about this project on the World Wide Web at **http://www.tcns.co.uk/chatback/**.

MY-VIEW

Subscription Address: listserv@sjuvm.stjohns.edu
List Address: MY-VIEW@sjuvm.stjohns.edu
Moderator's Address: Pat Davidson, **p.davidson@warwick.ac.uk**

Description: MY-VIEW is a global creative writing exchange for elementary school kids. Writing prompts are distributed to subscribers from around the world; for example, one prompt asked students to write about the view from their window. For older students or for those not responsive to this prompt, the assignment is altered to telling about your opinion on world events. All responses to the prompt are shared with project participants.

PENPAL-L

Subscription Address: listserv@unccvm.uncc.edu
List Address: penpal@unccvm.uncc.edu

Description: A listserv devoted to online pen-pal exchanges.

PHYSHARE

Subscription Address: listserv@psuvm.psu.edu
List Address: physhare@psuvm.psu.edu

Description: A list devoted to high school physics discussions and projects.

TALKBACK

Subscription Address: listserv@sjuvm.stjohns.edu
List Address: talkback@sjuvm.stjohns.edu

Description: A news exchange and discussion list for kids.

A Look Both Ways

E-mail listservs and newsgroups genuinely expand classroom boundaries, bringing the world to your students and vice versa. Yet not every situation or every project needs the diverse input of global exchange; as we shall see, sometimes just connecting your students with one another in the classroom is sufficient for a profound learning experience.

Just Connect

A variation on an old nursery rhyme provides the flavor of computer networks:

> One computer, two computer, three computer, four
>
> Five computer, six computer, seven computer, more...

And more and more and more—innumerable computers all hooked up to one another, capable of acting independently, yet also capable of sharing information simultaneously.

We used to think of *networking* as going somewhere to get to know other people in our fields, to talk with them, to "schmooze" with them, and to extend our professional knowledge and resources. Today, if you "network," you are more likely to be understood as referring to computer classrooms and the activities you can perform there.

Computer network technology is at the heart of the Internet. That's really all the Internet is—a lot of computers capable of being linked together. The difference between the Internet and your classroom is that, in the case of the latter, the connections between the computers is a physical one; in the case of the Internet, the connection is made via software and telephone lines.

 **Network:**
Two or more computers joined together with cabling to a server or host computer; two or more computers capable of "schmoozing." :)

Advantages of a Networked Classroom

For the most part, we learn in group settings, such as classrooms. From the earliest days of the American education system, with its image of the little red schoolhouse, we have learned in groups. Computer networking can reinvigorate small- and large-group pedagogies.

Networked Classrooms Facilitate Lecturing

Computers can greatly improve the efficacy of our class lectures. As we know, all too often students in the back rows can't see the blackboard and hear our words. Indeed, many take the opportunity during our lectures to catch up on their sleep, thus making it extremely unlikely that they will learn much. In addition, recent education research has demonstrated the vast differences in learning styles of students; using networked computers can help us target our lectures more effectively to many of these learning styles by incorporating multimedia and interactive lessons and exercises.

One of the greatest advantages of using networked computers is the ability to share files. I've found that one of the most useful techniques to lecture more effectively is to have a copy of my lecture on disk for students to refer to afterward. Many of our students are far better visual learners than aural. Often, material given in lectures is not processed well by our students. For whatever reasons (and there are many of them), students fail to differentiate primary information from secondary, or concepts from examples when processing information aurally.

Moreover, students are notoriously poor note-takers; by placing a file of lecture notes on the server, students can access the lecture material whenever they need to. In fact, I've taken this technological opportunity even further—I rarely lecture at all anymore. I assign my lectures along with the text reading on a given topic. Consequently, I have much more class time to devote to answering questions or having students work on projects that ask them to manipulate the material in some way—either through direct application of concepts, or through using the material in such higher-order, critical-thinking activities as analysis and synthesis.

Another advantage of networked computers for lecturing is the ability to use the computer as an overhead projector, much as you would use the blackboard in your class. I often prepare "slides" of key lecture points that I can display as I talk. If students have difficulty seeing the projection, I ask them to open the file at the computer.

There are several excellent presentation programs available to help you create your own lecture slides. PowerPoint, WordPerfect's Presentation, and Corel's CorelPresents are some good ones. You can even create slides in your favorite word processor if you don't care to invest a great deal of time learning new software.

Finally, using networked computers to lecture enables you to prepare multimedia lecture material to display, thereby reaching a wider variety of learners. You can include video clips, sound clips, text, and graphics in your lecture itself. Many companies are producing educational CD-ROMs and laser discs. Incorporating these materials into your own lectures is really quite simple; usually it's just a matter of telling the computer what drive to access when you give a command. This can be done well in advance of the class itself or even as you speak, provided you've got the material close at hand.

Networked Classrooms Facilitate Modeling

I spend a great deal of class time modeling thinking, reading, and writing activities for my students. One of the things I've noticed, to my chagrin, is that students never seem to take any notes during the modeling activity. I haven't figured out all of the reasons for their reluctance yet, but despite actually telling them what I'm doing and why, and that they should take notes, they simply don't. I'd like to think that my modeling activities are so interesting that the students are totally spellbound, but I strongly doubt it.

Networked environments again help enormously by allowing me to keep a permanent record of the activity in much the same way as a tape recorder or camcorder might. Instead of having tapes, however, I can write and type directly onto a computer linked to an overhead projector as I speak.

For example, if I'm modeling a kind of reading activity, I might prepare a computer presentation in advance that contains the kind of annotations I expect students to make as they read critically. These annotations would display on the computer projection (or on individual student screens in a computer classroom) as I read and spoke.

Long after the actual class, students would then be able to access the file(s) to refresh their memories. You might even consider having students respond to your annotations, thereby amassing a set of hypertextual critiques on a given reading.

Networked Classrooms Facilitate Class Discussion

I don't know about you, but I'm always struggling with how to make my classroom discussion activities more effective for all my students. I believe in discussion activities, and feel that they make learning more active for students and help them to internalize course concepts more effectively by having to verbalize them. Unfortunately, all too often class discussion is in fact a three- or four-way discussion between me and those already more verbal students. Small-group discussion, too, while engaging perhaps a few more students, often ends up becoming a dialogue among a handful of students.

Computer networking technology has been a godsend for enabling a more genuine and fruitful class discussion. The following discussion focuses on activities made possible by Interchange™, an integrated writing/discussion networked environment produced by the Daedalus Group (discussed later in this chapter). Check with your technical support staff for information about your school's software.

Conversations Have a Life of Their Own

Despite my best efforts, student conversations on a network often take on a life of their own, straying far from the assigned topic. Usually, I ignore off-topic conversations if students come back to the subject at hand. Sometimes, however, these conversations stray off into realms I would never have suspected. If the direction of the conversation seems fruitful, let it continue; if not, be prepared to intervene to get students back on track.

Shy Students Become More Active

In computer-networked discussions, students type their ideas at their own terminals, and their statements appear on everyone's screens. Many programs allow students to "log on" to the discussion using a pseudonym to disguise their identities. For a number of reasons, many students find this anonymity freeing. However, I generally allow my students to log on anonymously for the first two sessions at most; primarily because I want them to be and feel responsible for their verbal behaviors and ideas. Nonetheless, depending on your class and your objectives, you might well consider leaving these discussions anonymous.

I never cease to be amazed by these computer discussions; students who normally have little to say in class are suddenly quite verbal; the level of the discussions, too, are significantly higher than those held face-to-face. While in a class situation, many of the discussions have the quality of "pulling teeth" or "question-answer-silence" drills, our computer discussions are noisy, freewheeling, and often intensely heated.

Tip for Success Again, be prepared to intervene in the discussion directly. Students often get carried away in the course of a discussion and start being rude to their fellow conversants. Name-calling is rampant during these sessions.

Many students discover paper topics after an Interchange discussion; their involvement in the discussion and their feelings about it lead to a genuine desire to pursue an aspect of the debate. And as we all know, student-generated writing topics generally succeed far better than those we assign.

Small-Group Work Is More Easily Managed

I've long been an advocate of small-group discussion in my classes, but have always been concerned about how to handle off-task activity in groups. While I do walk around and sit in with all groups for a short time, I hate having to sit with groups for extended periods unless they're having problems. Moreover, every time I come over to a group, the conversation there stops dead.

By giving my students the benefit of the doubt, this situation interrupts the flow of potentially very good ideas at best and totally undercuts the group dynamic at worst.

Using a computer network for small-group discussions greatly alleviates this problem. In an integrated network environment such as Daedalus Interchange, students can talk in any "conference group" you create. For example, if I'm teaching a particular literary work, I might create up to four conferences for students to join based on questions about that literary work. Students can easily move from conference to conference, read their peers' ideas, and respond with their own. Figure 5.1 shows a typical Daedalus Interchange conference setup.

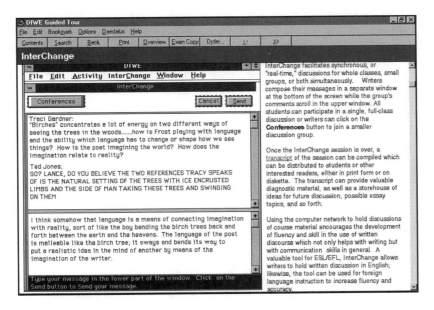

Fig. 5.1 A networked-based conference setup.

These computer-based conferences greatly reduce the amount of time spent by students discussing off-task subjects. Moreover, I can tell within minutes those students who are participating and those who are not. When I notice that a student is not participating in the discussion, I can intervene very quickly by either walking over to the student or sending a private message to that student.

115

"Conversations" Extend Beyond the Allotted Class Time

Because computer-based discussions are performed online, a permanent record of a discussion can be created and accessed by students. In my own classes, I always insist that students read over the discussion that evening for homework, and I assign several study questions about the transcript depending on the subject we're currently studying.

For example, if we're currently learning about ethos and its creation, I'll have students review the transcript and write a short description of one of the participants based on their perception of the writer's ethos. Or, if I allow students to use pseudonyms, I'll have students review the transcript and attempt to determine the identity of one of their classmates. See Network Project 5.1, "Who's Who," for a description of this activity.

The greatest advantage of networks for small-group discussion, however, is that students can extend the conversation outside of class. Often, I'll overhear my students discussing an Interchange session during lunch or in the hallways. For whatever reasons, conversing in this manner seems to engage students more strongly in course material. And as we all know, an engaged student generally indicates an active learner.

Students Teaching Students

Education research has convincingly demonstrated the increased motivation and learning that occurs when students are asked to "teach" other students, whether through a formal mentoring program or through informal tutoring, discussions, and group interactions. Students are also far more likely to listen to and accept what other students say than to what the teacher says. Networked computer software enhances student-to-student interaction, allows far greater possibilities for student sharing of information and papers, and enables you to have a record of ongoing interactions.

In a networked environment, student files are generally saved to a common area, thus allowing students access to one another's files. This file-sharing capability greatly facilitates collaborative learning and student mentoring activities. Students can access a single file, for example, and add their comments, ideas, and suggestions to it. Another student can then access the file and continue to develop the ideas.

For example, you might create an "India" disk in a geography class. Students would then contribute at least one idea or bit of information they gleaned from course readings or outside readings to that file. After a short period of time, you could have a fairly extensive disk of "India-related information." You might then suggest that students reflect and/or react to at least one of those pieces of information in a paragraph or two. Again, after a relatively short period of time, a growing body of different viewpoints will emerge about the numerous "facts" already recorded. Students can use this disk for a study guide, for brainstorming about paper topics, or as a "research source" in other activities. See Network Project 5.2, "Creating Your Own Encyclopedia," for a more extended description of this activity.

File-sharing capabilities also facilitate peer review of papers and projects. I, for one, really hate the time it takes away from lecture or activities for students to review one another's papers. All too often it seems that peer review is a waste of time; the quality of the students' feedback is generally poor despite a great amount of time spent on modeling and instruction. In a networked environment, I can have students review each other's work outside of class. Moreover, I have a record of student comments and writer revisions based on those comments.

Online Class Journaling

Another activity that benefits from networked computer environments is the standard journaling requirement many of us have in our classes. The benefit of having an online class journal as opposed to the individual journal is that students can collaborate with each other in producing the journal. We all know how uneven student responses to a journal requirement are. Many respond positively to the assignment by writing daily, while others simply don't see the point and don't know what to write at all.

With a class journal, however, most students become more engaged in the assignment, as they see an ever-growing body of viewpoints and ideas about the course material take shape. Moreover, class journals are more public, requiring a relatively formal and coherent discourse. These journals can be used as study guides for essay examinations, a topic resource for student papers and projects, or as a class "text" for analysis.

In my own classes, for example, I often use the class journal as the text for critical analysis exercises. Encourage your students to quote one another in their journal entries and papers. As time goes on, students learn what it means to participate in a community of learners; they experience the social construction of their knowledge and how that knowledge is negotiated and agreed upon.

Overview of Conferencing Software

Conferencing software is gradually becoming more available, as education software producers see the growing demand. Until very recently, only one or two packages existed; now, there are several from which to choose. Most conferencing packages come with extensive word processing features, online messaging capabilities, and mail.

The following discussion focuses on two conferencing packages: the Daedalus Integrated Writing Environment™ (DIWE) and Commonspace™, a collaborative writing software package. Every networking package is different, so some of the following applications may or may not be available on the software you use or choose.

Commonspace is a dedicated collaborative writing software package that is currently being expanded to include synchronous (real-time) communication capabilities. With this program, you and your students can comment on a draft. Each set of comments is contained in its own "column," thereby ensuring the integrity of the draft itself. Revisions to the original work are also saved in a separate column. By the end of the writing process, you have a complete history of a given document. Moreover, you can create several "workspaces."

One of the things I like to do with this software is to have students create their own Commonspace file for all their formal written work. I thus have all student papers in one file, each with their own set of comments, revisions, and changes. Figure 5.2 shows a typical Commonspace student file.

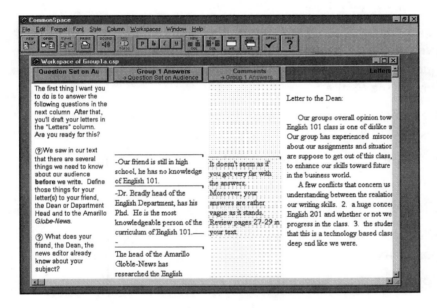

Fig. 5.2 The Commonspace writing software.

Figure 5.2 displays an audience exercise I have my first-year composition students complete. The first column contains a set of questions I prepared in advance. Students answered these questions in the second column. The third column contains my responses to the students' answers. Finally, the last column displays the first draft of a letter based on the information the students amassed in the second column. Later columns of the text contain my responses to their drafts, their revisions, and my final comments.

The DIWE software is a more flexible networking package, containing some eight components:

- Interchange, a real-time discussion function in which individuals compose messages and send them to all the members of the discussion group simultaneously.

- Mail, a LAN e-mail function.

- Write, a streamlined word processor.

- Invent, a brainstorming or prewriting tool that comes with 12 series of prompt questions from which to choose. You may customize these questions or create new prompts to suit specific courses and/or assignments (see Figure 5.3).

- Respond, a function that allows students to read online drafts and then respond to those drafts through a set of prompt questions you create.

- Bibliocite®, a database manager that allows writers to build a bibliography.

- Classmanager, a document manager.

- Classassignment, a one-way communication function that enables you to post daily assignments, general announcements, and more.

While it can be used with almost every subject, DIWE is a flexible comprehensive writing and invention package, particularly for the networked English composition classroom. One of the most useful portions of the package, along with Interchange, is the Invent module. Figure 5.3 shows a typical Invent screen with a writing/thinking prompt about secondary sources. While the module comes with an initial set of prompts, you can create your own as well.

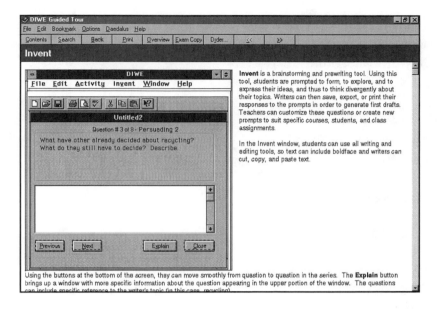

Fig. 5.3   The Invent module of DIWE.

Addresses of Major Vendors

For more information about available network software and products, contact the following:

Commonspace
Sixth Floor Media
A Houghton Mifflin Group
222 Berkeley St.
Boston, MA 02116
Voice: (800) 565-6247
Fax: (800) 565-6236
http://www.sixthfloor.com
Commonspace: **http://www.sixthfloor.com/Products/CS/CS.html**
e-mail: **info@sixthfloor.com**

Daedalus Integrated Writing Environment (DIWE)
The Daedalus Group, Inc.
1106 Clayton Lane, Suite 250W
Austin, TX 78723
Voice: (512) 459-0637
Fax: (512) 452-5206
http://www.daedalus.com
Integrated Writing Package: **http://www.daedalus.com/info/diwe**
diwe_info.html
e-mail: **info@daedalus.com**

Norton Textra Connect™
W. W. Norton & Company, Inc.
500 Fifth Avenue
New York, NY 10110
Voice: (212) 354-5500
Fax: (212) 869-0856
For user support, pricing, and general information, contact Fred McFarland at 800-533-7904.
http://www.wwnorton.com/connect.htm
e-mail: **fmcfarland@wwnorton.com**

Teaching Students to "Network"

There isn't much to teaching students how to be comfortable in computer network environments; they seem to take to it quite readily. The bulk of training surrounds teaching students where and how to access and save their work.

Network Project 5.1:
Who's Who

Subject: English, social studies

Grade Level: 4 through 12

Description: This project asks students to carefully review network transcripts to determine the culture or identity of another student.

Objective: To help students develop a sense of how they communicate their identities and personalities through writing; to help foster student sensitivity to cultural, regional, and individual difference.

Procedure:

1. Set up a number of network conferences in advance according to the particular procedure associated with your network software.

2. Divide students into groups depending on the number of conferences you've set up.

3. Have students log onto the network conference using pseudonyms. Tell students that their pseudonyms should try to "say something" about them—their favorite TV personality, cartoon character, or cultural background.

4. Have students engage in discussion about their cultural backgrounds or family histories.

5. After the conference, print out or save to disk transcripts of the conferences for each group.

6. For homework and the next class discussion, students should attempt to guess the "real" identity of one of their conference participants, using the transcript for clues and evidence.

Variations: This project can be varied in numerous ways, according to your pedagogical demands. You can, for example, have students examine the way(s) in which authority was established in the discussions—whose voice(s) became dominant and why. Alternatively, you can have students discuss the way(s) in which their pseudonyms affected student response to one another.

Other variations can be introduced in the conference content. Consider having each group represent a country students are studying. The students could describe their country's major characteristics; other students would then "guess" what countries participated. Another variation might be to assign student groups to particular positions about an issue. Students might then discuss the points at issue that arose in the discussion as well as identify places at which the discussions broke down or reached consensus.

> **⇄ Tip for Success** This project works extremely well with younger students. The primary tasks for a successful outcome are to make sure the students stay on topic for a reasonable amount of time and make sure you include elements from the electronic discussion in your followup, whether by an exam or lecture. Students need to know that their comments are important to the course and subject.

Network Project 5.2:
Creating Your Own Encyclopedia

Subject: All

Grade-level: K through 12

Description: Students are asked to compile information about the subject being studied to a "master disk."

Objective: To help students master course content material; to help empower students with respect to their own learning.

Procedure:

1. Format and label a disk for all students to use. For very young students, you will probably want to compile the information to disk yourself.

2. If the topic is broad and/or complex, divide the students into groups and assign each group a specific portion of the topic. For example, if the topic is another culture, you might assign student groups to cover different aspects of that culture.

3. Tell students that they must contribute to the class "encyclopedia" at least once a week. Their input can take many forms: summaries of class readings, abstracts and references to outside readings, pictures, and descriptions of specific items.

4. Check periodically to make sure all students are participating.

5. Whenever possible, incorporate student-generated information and ideas into class content and discussion.

6. At the end of the unit, have students create a copy of the master disk or print out the information for use in their studying.

Network Project 5.3:
The Online Class Journal

Subject: All

Grade-level: 4 through 12

Description: Similar to the previous project, this activity asks students to contribute regularly to an ongoing discussion about course content and related issues.

Objective: To help students integrate diverse viewpoints; to help empower students with respect to their own learning.

Procedure:

1. Prepare and label a master disk to store journal activity or designate a file on the server for students to use.

2. Tell students that they must contribute to the class journal at least once a week.

3. Students should begin by stating their own positions and ideas. Thereafter, give students a choice whether to begin a new topic or to respond to an earlier entry.

4. To the extent possible, incorporate ideas from the class journal into your class lecture or discussion activities.

Networking with One or Two Computers

If your school hasn't yet obtained the funds to install a fully networked computer classroom, all hope is not lost. You can still devise exercises that simulate a networked environment, even if you only have one or two computers available at your school. It's not as easy to manage and takes some planning, ingenuity, and just plain stick-to-it-iveness, but it can be done.

With only one or two computers, you can still simulate electronic conferencing. You can, for example, have students respond to questions and save their responses on a single disk. After one student responds, she passes the disk to another member of her group. That person responds and passes the disk on to the next member and so on, until all have responded. Students can then make a copy of the disk with everyone's responses for themselves.

Another possibility is to simulate peer review sessions by having students exchange disks with one another to respond and comment upon each other's work. Yet another possibility is to have students collaborate on a piece of writing that deals with an issue in your field. In this exercise, one student may start off by writing an introduction with a clear thesis statement. The next student may provide a paragraph or two in support of that idea. The third student may provide a paragraph that illustrates the concepts provided by the previous student, and so on.

If your students are very young, consider having them add a sentence or two instead of paragraphs. In a relatively short time, students can create a coherent group paper that documents their stance on an issue.

Extending Your Repertoire

Batson, Trent; Bass, Randy. "Teaching and learning in the computer age: Primacy of Process." *Change* 28.2 (1996): 42.

——————. "ENFI Research." *Computers and Composition* 10.3 (Aug 1993): 93-101.

————————. "The ENFI Project: An Update." *Teaching English to Deaf and Second-Language Students* 6.2 (Fall 1988): 5-8.

————————. "A Selective National Survey of ENFI Real-Time Conferencing in the Composition Classroom." Paper presented at the Annual Meeting of the Conference on College Composition and Communication (40th, Seattle, WA, March 16-18, 1989).

Cornish, Maria; Monahan, Brian. "A Network Primer for Educators." *Educational Technology* 36.2 (Mar-Apr 1996): 55-57.

Daly, Kevin F. "A Planning Guide for Instructional Networks, Part I." *Computing Teacher* 22.1 (Sep 1994): 11-12, 14-15.

DiMatteo, Anthony. "Under Erasure: A Theory for Interactive Writing in Real Time." *Computers and Composition* 7 (special issue, April 1990): 71-84.

ERIC. "Computer Networking." *Eric Review* 4.1 (Fall 1995).

————. "Connecting K-12 Schools to the Information Superhighway." 1995.

Kemp, Fred. "Who Programmed This? Examining the Instructional Attitudes of Writing-Support Software." *Computers and Composition* 10.1 (Nov 1992): 9-24.

————————. "Computer Writing Environments: Theory, Research, and Design, Bruce Britton and Shawn M. Glynn." *College composition and communication* 41.3 (October 1990): 339-341.

Lederman, Tim. "Local Area Networks for K-12 Schools." ERIC Digest. Nov 1995.

Long, Thomas L.; Pedersen, Christine. "Critical Thinking about Literature through Computer Networking." Paper presented at the Annual Computer Conference of the League for Innovation in the Community College (9th, Orlando, FL, October 21-24, 1992).

Moeller, Babette, et. al. "Using Network Technology to Create New Writing Environments for Deaf Students: Teachers' Strategies and Student Outcomes." Paper presented at the Biennial Meeting of the Society for Research in Child Development (60th, New Orleans, LA, March 25-28, 1993).

Norales, Francisca O. "Networking: A Necessary Component in a Computer-Literacy Course." *Collegiate Microcomputer* 11.4 (Nov 1993): 259-263.

Perone, Karen. "Networking CD-ROMs: A Tutorial Introduction." *Computers in Libraries* 16.2 (Feb 1996): 71-77.

A Look Both Ways

The educational potential of networking is phenomenal. For the first time in history, we have the opportunity to cooperate and collaborate with others from around the globe on a daily basis—in writing! This century has witnessed a renaissance in communication technology, the likes of which have never been possible before. As we shall see in forthcoming chapters, we can actually "talk" to people from around the world with the same speed that the telephone provides.

6

Conversing with the World

Computers are truly a marvelous invention. To think that the words I type on a keyboard can be seen by others hundreds and thousands of miles away—immediately! I can hold a conversation with a colleague in Illinois about a planned collaborative article; I can meet with numerous colleagues to discuss the latest *Chronicle*; I can meet and talk with hundreds of others to wile away a Sunday afternoon.

Like having a telephone conversation, chatting is a fairly rapid verbal exchange. Everyone's words appear on all participants' monitors and several conversations may take place simultaneously. Thus, it is differentiated from e-mail in that it is a *synchronous* (at the same time) rather than an *asynchronous* form of communication.

 **Chat:**
A synchronous, real-time communication activity; a kaffee-klatch.

Chatting Is Halfway Between Speaking and Writing

All of the benefits we've seen from using e-mail and networks in classrooms are evident in using chat technology as well. Our students have grown up in a world that privileges talk over writing; they feel far less threatened when asked to speak their responses than to write them. Chat technology makes the best of both worlds—students feel as though they are speaking, when, in fact, they must write to verbalize their thoughts.

While *speaking* through the written word, chatting will probably never improve a student's ability to write extended coherent discourses. Nonetheless, it does provide a means to improve a student's attitude about writing. For numerous reasons, students feel alienated from writing, seeing it as something they must do in school or for English classes. Writing is associated with work rather than play, with pleasing someone rather than communicating. Chatting goes far toward changing these negative attitudes; writing becomes simply something one does to interact with others.

Chatrooms Provide Immediate Feedback

While participating in a chatroom feels like speaking, it is in fact writing. People respond to written statements. Students can tell immediately if something they've "said" has been misinterpreted or needs further elaboration.

 **Chatroom:**
A chat channel you can join to talk with other people.

Chatrooms Provide Spaces for Online Consultations

All too often student writing is left unresponded to for substantial periods of time—often up to a week. While it is generally impossible to comment upon student work within 24 hours, chatrooms provide a forum for student-teacher interaction outside the classroom. One advantage to meeting with students in a chatroom to discuss their papers is that you need not *grade* the paper prior to the meeting. You need only be able to respond to the paper, thus greatly reducing the interval between student submission and teacher response. As we know, speed of response is a student motivator.

Chatrooms Expand the Classroom

As with e-mail, chatrooms greatly expand the classroom boundaries. Your students can meet with one another during study halls or in the evening online to help one another with homework and understanding course content. Moreover, your students can meet with other students from around the world in a chatroom. Again, the great advantage of using chat technology is its instant response nature. Students need not wait for a response to their questions or comments as in e-mail; the interaction is immediate.

Moreover, chat technology greatly facilitates collaboration. Students can discuss their projects almost as effectively as they can face to face. You can even have students collaborate on projects with those other students far away. See Assignment 6.1, "Working with Others," later in this chapter for details on how to do this.

Chat Technology Helps Shy Students

As we saw in the previous chapter, shy students can greatly benefit from using chat technology. Many students fear the attention that speaking up can bring; chat technology allows those students to have their say by removing the face-to-face component. Moreover, as in networking, students can choose nicknames rather than use their own names.

Inside Chat Programs

There are a number of chat programs, but they're all designed to do one thing—connect to a central server. The most common chat program is mIRC, a very inexpensive shareware program. In the United States there are some 10 servers running the program, the largest located at **us.undernet.org**. Most chat programs come with the servers already listed and configure your computer to go directly to one of them when you start the program. Thus, for most programs, it is simply a matter of pointing and clicking to connect to a chat server.

Obtaining the software is really quite easy; you just point your browser to your favorite software spot (**http://www.tucows.com** is a really good place for software) and click the appropriate icon. Chat programs are generally listed under icons called "Chat," "Text Chat," or "IRC." Clicking the icon generally retrieves about 10 to 20 programs. Click the one you want to download. Make sure you have some good reading material or a computer with a good deal of memory—downloading software can sometimes take as long as an hour.

Finding a Channel and Joining a Discussion

Currently, there are about 5,000 registered chatrooms. You used to be able to see them all when connecting to the chat server; now, because there are so many, you need to use the list command, /list, to see them.

When you use the /list command, you should see a list of names preceded by a # sign, as shown in Figure 6.1.

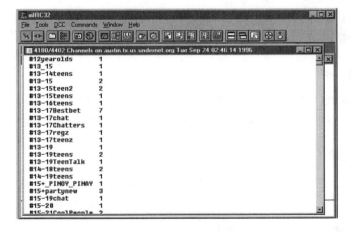

Fig. 6.1   The results of a /list command.

To join a channel you see listed, simply type

   /join #<*channel*>

When you join a channel, a window similar to the one shown in Figure 6.2 opens.

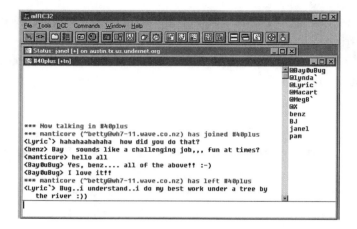

Fig. 6.2 A typical chatroom window.

Talking in a chatroom is as simple as just typing what you want to say. Often, however, you'll want to express some emotion or perform some action in response to someone's statements. To do that, simply type

> **/me** *<message or action>*

substituting what you want to do for the part in the angle brackets. Thus, if I wanted to indicate that someone's statement made me laugh, I would type

> **/me laughs**

The message "Jane laughs" would appear in the chat window.

> **Note** You'll notice from the preceding discussion that all chat commands begin with a /.

Starting a Chat Discussion

If none of the current discussions in the chat list match up with your needs, you can start another chat discussion by simply typing

> **/join #<chatroom title>**

substituting the name of the discussion you want. If I brought my students for an online chat discussion, I would first log on before them and set up a chatroom by typing

> **/join #English100**

The chat program would see that no current chatroom existed named *English100* and one would be created. Because I named it, I become the chatroom sysop, in charge of that room.

 **Sysop:**
Short for systems operator.

Controlling Your Chatroom

A powerful chat command, /mode, allows you to specify certain parameters for your chatroom. You can, for example, set it up so that it's a private room, accessible to others by invitation only. I recommend setting the room up in this fashion so that others connecting to the chat software cannot join your channel inadvertantly. To do this, simply type

> **/mode #<channelname> +i**

See Tables 6.1 and 6.2 for common IRC commands and basic sysop commands.

Chatting Should Be Closely Monitored

Because of the global, easy-access nature of chatrooms, you need to closely monitor student activity. Most of the bad press Internet activity has received stems from chatrooms. Because people get to use nicknames, it's difficult to tell whether someone belongs in a particular chatroom or not. Moreover, many chatrooms are dedicated to nonacademic discussions—that's both their advantage and disadvantage.

When taking students to a chatroom, you do need to watch their activity. Many of my students will leave the room to check out other chatrooms. That's fine, if our class is devoted to learning how to chat; otherwise, I want my students on task in our discussion. You can easily tell whether a student leaves the chatroom—his or her nickname disappears from the list of active participants on the right side of the window (refer to Figure 6.2).

Table 6.1   Basic IRC Commands

Command	*Explanation*
/invite *<nickname>#<channelname>*	Invites a user to join your channel
/join #*<channelname>*	Join the specified channel
/list	List all currently available channels
/me *<message>*	Tells everyone what you are doing or feeling
/msg *<nickname><message>*	Sends a private message to the specified user
/part #*<channelname>*	Leave the specified channel

Command	Explanation
/whois <nickname>	Shows information about the specified user
/quit	Disconnects you from the IRC server

Table 6.2   Basic Mode Commands

Mode Character	Explanation
b <nickname>	Bans someone from your channel
i	Sets channel to invite-only
m	Channel is moderated; only channel operators can talk
o <nickname>	Makes someone a channel operator
p	Sets channel to private
s	Sets channel to secret (hidden from /l listings; accessible only by a secret key)
k <key>	Sets the secret key for a secret channel

Sample Mode Commands

While the above listing may seem confusing at first, it's really simple after you get the hang of it. To ban someone who barges into your chatroom, for example, you merely type

/mode #<channelname> +b <nickname>

Thus I would type

> **/mode #English100 +b bigboy**

to banish bigboy from the room.

To set my channel to private, I would type

> **/mode #English100 +p**

To "undo" any previously set modes, you simply type the same thing using a minus sign rather than the plus. Thus, to allow bigboy back to the channel discussion, I would type

> **/mode #English100 -b bigboy**

Many, many more IRC commands are available. Check the online help system that comes with most chat programs for complete listings. The commands listed in this chapter, however, are sufficient for most of what you might want to do with chatrooms in your teaching.

Teaching Students to Chat

Chatrooms can be used for different kinds of meetings. Assignment 6.1 and Project 6.2 detail how to introduce students to the online community of "chatters," and offers suggestions to help students make sense of their experiences.

Assignment 6.1:
Working with Others

The following assignment is adapted from one developed by Dr. Becky Rickly at the University of Michigan.

Subject: All

Grade-level: 7-12

Description: Students should write a short paper analyzing an electronic discussion community. The analysis should address the rules of the group (who talks, who listens), the group's function (what is discussed, what is learned), and the group's dynamics (how many different people participate over a period of time, what kinds of roles are played by different people, what is the relationship between males and females).

Objective: To help students become familiar with the world of synchronous electronic communication; to help students master the skills of analysis and synthesis.

Preparation: Prepare a handout on basic IRC commands and take your students to the computer classroom for a practice session or two.

Procedure:

1. In an assignment handout, identify how many times and for how long you want your students to participate or watch IRC discussions. For example, state that students must participate in five channel discussions for at least 30 minutes each.

2. In an assignment handout, target the kind of questions you'd like students to think about and then model the kind of thinking that goes into analysis.

   a. How well do the participants already seem to know each other? How can you tell when participants are or are not already acquainted?

   b. How are newcomers received into a particular discussion? Are they welcomed? Are they shut out? Are you welcomed or shut out in any of the discussions?

   c. What kinds of rules are at work in each discussion? What kind of verbal standards are maintained on the channel? How are they maintained?

   d. Do smaller communities exist within any larger discussions? What kind of community dynamics exist?

e. Because IRC is a purely visual medium, participants must rely almost entirely on language to convey their personalities. In what ways do you see individual personalities expressed? How are you using language to express your own personality?

f. Does the anonymity of the participants alter how they react to one another, including yourself and other participants?

g. How do you see community formation within the IRC setting?

h. How does an IRC community differ from other communities in which face-to-face interaction occurs?

Tip for Success This assignment can vary significantly to adapt to different technologies. If your school doesn't have an IRC program, you can alter the assignment to investigate your local network discussions (see Chapter 5, "Just Connect"), e-mail listserv discussions (see Chapter 4, "Continuing the Conversations"), or MOO discussions (see Chapter 7, "'MOOving' Right Along").

IRC Project 6.2:
Extending the Boundaries

Subject: All

Grade-level: 7-12

Description: Students collaborate with those from another class, school, or region to produce papers or another kind of project.

Objective: To help students learn to interact responsibly with others via electronic communication.

Preparation:

1. Well in advance, contact another teacher you know who wants to incorporate computer-mediated communication into the classroom. (Or, if you don't know anyone, join one of the listservs mentioned in Chapter 4 and ask.)

2. Work closely with that teacher for several months developing the kind of project you want your students to undertake. This project could take the form of written papers, brochures, information handouts, musical compositions, or just about anything. Make sure you feel comfortable with the other teacher, particularly whether you feel he is committed to the project. Students need a lot of pushing under the best of circumstances; in collaborative projects such as these, both teachers must be willing to devote a lot of time to overseeing student work.

3. Prepare assignment sheets for students.

Procedure:

1. Break students up into small groups of no more than four.

2. Pair up your student groups with the student groups from the other class.

3. Designate times for each group to meet with their counterparts from the other class on IRC.

4. Students should develop their projects together via IRC, e-mail ongoing drafts to the other students in their groups, and meet periodically with the group via IRC to discuss changes, revisions, and other ideas that affect the project.

A Look Both Ways

Computer networking is one of the best tools technology offers. The ability for people to talk and work with others far away greatly increases student involvement. Most of the work done thus far surrounds investigating the way(s) that using computer-mediated communication changes our ways of working and our attitudes toward that work.

Much work is also being done that looks at the way(s) Computer-Mediated Communication (CMC) is slowly changing our writing and speech. Obviously, such studies will be very long-term, but even now certain patterns are emerging. CMC requires a kind of thought-speech somewhere between speaking and more formal writing. CMC also brings greatly extended opportunities for confronting difference and, with any luck, will help us to establish more lasting and genuine global peace.

Yet global conversations are limited in their pedagogical applications (as is any specific pedagogical tool). As we'll see in the next chapter, there exists another set of computer technologies—MOO technology—that extends yet further the possibilities of active learning and collaboration in computer environments.

"MOOving" Right Along

Imagine you're Socrates sitting in prison waiting to appear before the Senate reflecting, as always, about the world around you. How to convince them of your innocence? You pick up the quill and ink they've left you for solace during your long hours of confinement. Slowly, carefully, you begin to write. But wait! You hear the loud echoes of the guards' heavy steps coming toward your cell. They bind you and hurt you as they push you toward the door. One guard glances at the paper you've left on the table. "Guilty," it states. Guilty of the most heinous of human crimes—the passion for truth.

Imagine. You stand there, burning with desire, burning with the heat of the words that waft through the smoke-filled air. "They have no right," you think; "they don't understand." The crowd is starting to push forward, their desire for fulfillment so strong it physically starts to push you toward your destiny. You whimper as the minister's hard, harsh words burn into your brain, more painful even than the small darts of flame that yearn to burn your flesh. "Witch," he cries out, jabbing his long, craggy finger into your flesh. "Burn," he commands, as they tie you to the stake. As if fueled by the crowd's desire, the flames rise to caress you. Your knowledge of the even hotter flames that await the Salem citizens gives you the strength to endure to the end.

Imagine. Yes, imagine. That's what lies at the heart of MOO technology. The ability to create worlds from words, out of the raw "stuff" of imagination.

A MOO by Any Other Name

MOOs are virtual spaces capable of being built, inhabited, and programmed by several users at once. In the early days, they were known as MUDs, Multi-User Domains (or Dimensions), or Dungeons, and were used primarily for game-playing of the Dungeons and Dragons type. As time went on, MUDs were expanded to other applications and became known as MUSHes (Multi-User Shared Hallucinations), and, now, as MOOs

(Multi-User Object-Oriented Dimensions). Although the learning curve is somewhat high, the potential of MOOs for helping students learn is well worth the time and effort.

Tip for Success Despite a rapid emergence of the use of MOOs for educational purposes, many people still see them as primarily for games. Make sure you get permission from your supervisors to use MOOs in your classroom.

The Best of All Worlds: Combining Networking with Building/Programming

Just as with chat and network technologies, MOOs work well for the rapid exchange of information. Again, like the previous technologies, they are synchronous environments, designed for real-time interactions. But the programming capability of MOOspace greatly expands the power of these cyber-interactions for student learning.

In addition to talking, MOOs are spaces for active learning, allowing students to construct models of course content material, to collaborate with other students from around the world on projects, and to build huge imaginative worlds peopled with programmed objects around the material of a particular unit.

Brainstorming with the Whole Class

MOOs work in much the same way as chatrooms and are ideal for brainstorming sessions. Words that you type on your keyboard appear on the MOO, visible to all who are in the room with you. (MOOspace is generally divided up into rooms, similar to the way chat conversations are assigned virtual spaces called "rooms.")

Consequently, you can have your students meet with one another at a MOO to discuss ideas, answer questions, and brainstorm topics for papers. You can even keep strangers out of your conversations on the MOO, simply by locking the door of the room you're in. Just as in a room full of people, you can hold a private conversation in a MOO by whispering to another person or by paging them. "MOO Assignment 7.2: Online Class Discussion" helps students become familiar with working on a MOO.

Collaborating with Others

Because of its synchronous nature, MOOspace provides a terrific venue for collaborating with others. Used in conjunction with e-mail, these technologies are powerful tools for group projects.

Almost all the work I do these days is collaborative; almost all the work I do is accomplished using MOO technology. For example, in the last year I have extended my collegial network by hundreds. Starting in 1994, I began to attend the weekly MOO sessions at MediaMOO, not-so-imaginatively called "The Tuesday Night Café." This weekly meeting is attended by dozens of my colleagues in the field of rhetoric and composition. We discuss current issues in composition theory, classroom successes and failures, share ideas about our classroom practices, and socialize. Every Tuesday evening. Even better, I don't have to go out in freezing, snowy weather to attend these; I merely turn on my computer and I'm there.

One of my favorite sessions is devoted to brainstorming topics and ideas for upcoming conferences. Instead of trying to come up with program proposals on my own, I have dozens of other heads out there to think with. Even more fun, I have others to collaborate with on those panels, presentations, and papers. With the advent of MOO technology, I never have to work totally alone again. And it doesn't cost a dime! What luxury.

The Collaborative Process

MOOspace can be used at all stages of the writing and learning processes, from brainstorming, to drafting, to reviewing and editing. Several of my students have often met together in the MOO to work on their collaborative projects.

How often have we, as teachers, faced student resistance to working in groups? "There's not enough time" or "our schedules are different" or "I don't have transportation" are common student responses to our demands that they work with others in their class. With the advent of MOO technology, students no longer can use those excuses quite so blithely.

With only a fairly good computer and a modem, students can work together even when they're all at home. Perhaps not all students have the necessary hardware at home right now, but shortly most will have. "MOO Assignment 7.3: Online Peer Review" describes how students can use the MOO to work in peer groups.

MOOspace also can be used to have students work collaboratively with classes from around the world. These collaborative projects do take some preparation on your part—at least at the beginning. Students often become so excited at meeting and talking with others from around the globe that they forget they are there to work. Monitor student activity closely. See "MOO Project 7.1: Working with Others" for a good collaborative MOO activity.

Illustrating the Power of Language

We give lip service to such truisms as "the pen is mightier than the sword," although "sticks and stones can break my bones but words can never harm me," is probably more characteristic of today's attitude toward language. Somewhere in time we lost our faith in language as a real power in the world. MOOs can do much to change this attitude and restore our youth's faith in the efficacy of language.

MOOspace is text. That's all it is. Nothing there has any physical substance. Within that universe, however, people can perform actions as real as those they perform in other aspects of their daily lives. The difference is that you must use words to perform all actions. Consequently, MOOspace is one of the safest places on this planet, a space for children to learn the consequences of their behaviors—physical and verbal—without fear of actually damaging something.

Several examples here might help. In order to do anything in MOOspace, you must type in a command. Thus, in order to walk out of a room, you must type **walk**. One of the best class discussions I had with students arose from this fact. One of the students thought it was "neat" that words in a MOO caused change, caused an action. In MOOspace, you might have or carry a sword, but you need to know words to be able to wield it.

There is, of course, a downside to this. About a year ago, I brought some students to the MOO to meet with another class from Arizona. My students went wild; they got so excited at the idea that they were actually talking to people who lived two states away. Words raced by on the screen. Students were doing the typographical equivalent of yelling, throwing things, and generally being obnoxious. Both groups got into the fray; the result was a giant imaginary virtual electric sausage fight between the two groups of students.

It took quite a while for both of us teachers to settle the students down enough to get them to log off! I learned a great deal about preparing students for MOOing before bringing them on. I now provide my students with copious handouts on MOO etiquette before ever bringing them online.

We left the MOO, and I insisted they print out copies of the session. The following class, we had a long heart-to-heart discussion about what had happened. We talked about how everyone felt before, during, and after the "sausage fight." We reached the conclusion that as far as feelings were concerned, there was no difference between the action on the MOO and had it taken place in the classroom. Students left that class very quietly; I think they learned the hard lesson that words can indeed harm you.

I realize this example is negative and runs the risk of making you reluctant to use MOO technology in your classes. I can only assure you that such things happen very rarely. Moreover, not all of life's lessons are happy ones. You need to be prepared—and to prepare your students—for some very real and intense experiences when you venture to MOO.

Cyberlife is not a protection from daily life; it is as fallible a space as the humans that inhabit it. We can be grateful, though, that experiences such as these take place virtually and *not* in the playground. The students in both these classes left chastened and upset with their verbal behavior. I know they left far wiser and more knowledgeable about the power of language.

Learning About Ethos

Because MOOs are text-based environments, students must create and describe their MOO "character" through text. I know my students have a difficult time understanding the concept of ethos—the writer's personality on paper—both how to create an effective ethos for a specific audience and how to recognize an author's ethos. Bringing them to a MOO brings this concept alive for students.

One of the first things MOO etiquette requires is the creation of a substantial description of yourself. This description need not correspond to "reality." Many women I know, for example, have chosen male genders for their MOO character. I sometimes have my students create a number of descriptions for themselves, interacting on the MOO as that character for a certain amount of time.

We spend time in class talking about their experience as different characters—in what ways their behaviors changed, their feelings changed, differences in the way(s) people responded to them when they had a different character. Students who were having difficulty understanding how to create a character in their writing suddenly blossomed in their ability to adapt their personality to different audiences. "MOO Assignment 7.4, Creating Your Character" describes this activity in more detail.

Building Text-Based Models of Course Content

The real power of a MOO becomes evident when students learn enough to start creating objects on a MOO. We've long known that people learn more when actively engaged with the subject matter. MOOs provide a tool for students to create virtual models of course content material.

For example, suppose you're teaching a unit on biology. Students could go to the MOO and re-create a text-based model of protozoa or the cosmic soup. In chemistry, students could build atoms and stage chemical reactions. In history, students could build re-creations of battles or historical figures.

One Canadian MOO, WaldenPond, is structured around the 18th century. "Rooms" are built thematically around the social and political events during the century. At another MOO, literature students have built a re-creation of Dante's *Inferno*, complete down to seven levels.

The possibilities are limitless. Students don't just hear a lecture and regurgitate material: they must have a genuine understanding of the material to put it to use in a MOO. Even better, since MOOs are text-based, their writing skills are constantly at work when building and creating objects in a MOO.

Building a Virtual Classroom

When I took my first steps into MOOspace, I discovered I was quite the realist and a conservative to boot. I felt I needed—and my students would desire—a space that resembled a traditional classroom as much as possible. So I spent a good deal of time creating a space that looked exactly like a traditional classroom. There were six tables with chairs to sit at, a blackboard, a notice board, a teacher's desk, a bookshelf, a projector, and a clock.

As I learned more about the capabilities of MOOspace, I added Ichabot, the story-telling robot, and Graham, a grammar robot ("bot" in MOOspeak). These virtual classrooms have all the virtues of traditional classrooms, and then some.

As in a traditional classroom, students can sit at the small tables to do small-group work. One advantage of a MOO classroom is that you can restrict conversation and action output to just those people at a particular table. In other words, when students sit at particular tables, what they say and do will be "heard" only by the other students at the same table and not by the whole room. This becomes an extremely important capability for teaching when you recall that all words typed in a MOO are seen by everyone else in the same room.

Another advantage of a MOO classroom is that you can "log" the class, produce a written transcript of everything that takes place during class. Such a capability takes class discussion to another level. Students can discuss a concept during class, e-mail themselves a transcript of the discussion, read and analyze the discussion, and discuss it in the next class.

Imagine, all those terrific ideas that come out of small-group discussions are no longer ephemeral. They can be recalled and extended and developed over time. See "Creating Your Classroom" later in this chapter for extensive details on building your MOO Classroom.

Basic MOO Concepts

When you first become a registered character on a MOO, you need to familiarize yourself with the rules and regulations of that particular MOO. I've got a classroom and an office at Diversity University MOO (DU), a MOO primarily devoted to educational uses. The examples and discussions that follow are based on my experience there; slight variations will arise at other MOOs, although they all derive from the same core program.

MOOs are administrated by a group of people known as "wizards." When you first get started, make sure you contact the wizards and let them know what you want to do on the MOO. They are there to help you in every way they can.

Connecting to a MOO

MOO connections are made using a telnet connection (see Chapter 1). However, there are several inexpensive shareware programs that are designed for MOO interactions. The problem with a "raw" telnet connection is that all the output from the MOO scrolls down the screen, even as you type your input.

This can be very confusing for "newbies." MOO client software generally provides two windows—one for typing your input and one for viewing the conversation. Figure 7.1 shows a typical MOO client screen.

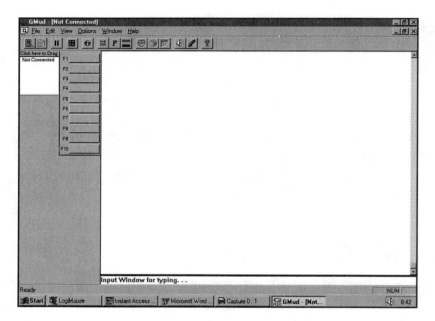

Fig. 7.1 MOO client screen.

TECH TALK **Newbies:**
People new to Internet MOO technology; antonym of "oldbies."

When the program first makes the connection to the MOO, a screen, similar to the one shown in Figure 7.2 with basic MOO commands for connecting, should appear.

As Figure 7.2 shows, you need to type a "connect" command (co) to get onto the MOO. Until you have a permanent character, you will have to connect as a guest. To do that, follow the directions on the screen or type

co guest

Because you're participating on a computer program, make sure to remember to log off the MOO when you're done by typing **@quit**. Logging off helps keep the MOO database current and "clean."

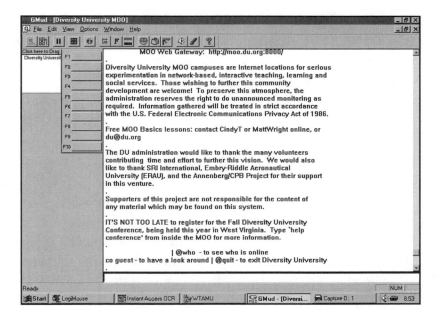

Fig. 7.2 Connecting to a MOO.

When you make a telnet connection to a MOO, you should first set the page length and line lengths to conform to your monitor size and window. Otherwise, too much or too little text will appear for easy reading. To do this, you use the pagelength, linelength, and word wrap commands as follows:

@**pagelength 24**
@**linelength 80**
@**wrap on**

If these settings don't work, adjust the numeric values up or down until a comfortable amount of text appears on your screen.

Looking Around on a MOO

Everything in a MOO is stored in a computer's memory and thus has an "object number." For example, although I go by "Jane" at the MOO, the computer knows me as #9881. According to the computer, everything in a MOO is really only one of three things—a character object, a location or room object, or a "thing" object.

Thus, everything on a MOO has an object number, a "name" or "alias" it goes by, and a description property that identifies it. That's why it's so important when you first log onto a MOO to describe yourself. Other people can then "look" at you and see how you identify yourself. To describe yourself, you use the @describe command as follows:

@describe me as <*text*>

This will set the description property of your character object. For example, my MOO description is something like this:

Jane #9881

An English teacher who one day hopes to build and inhabit the virtual spaces she loves the most. You can recognize her by her Cheshire cat-like grin that just keeps growing. If you don't watch out, you just might get caught up in that grin.

One of the most useful commands on a MOO is look. Typing look will retrieve information about the place on the MOO you're located in, the people who are there in the room, and the location and direction of the room's exits. Figure 7.3 shows a typical result of the MOO's look command.

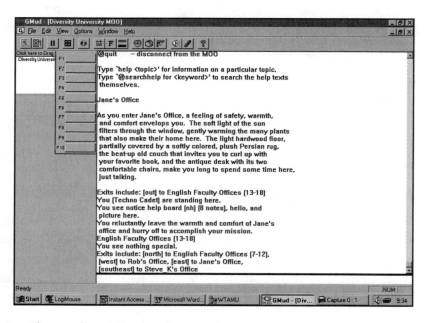

Fig. 7.3 The results of "looking" around on a MOO.

You also can "look" at every object in a MOO room using the look command merely by typing

look *<object>*

Thus, you can type **look Jane** to see my description or **look blackboard** to see what's written there.

Although MOOs can be quite complex environments, a few simple commands will suffice for most things you and your students might want to do there. Table 7.1 explains these commands.

Table 7.1   Basic MOO Commands

Command	*Description*
look	Retrieve information about your location
say (or ")	Talk to the other people in the room with you
emote (or :)	Communicate an action or emotion to others in the room with you
page	Talk privately with a person in another room from you
whisper (or mu)	Whisper privately to someone in the room with you
@go	Teleport to another MOO room
@join *<name>*	Teleport to that player's location on the MOO
@quit	Log off the MOO
@who	Retrieve a list of currently logged-in people
help	Access the MOO help system

Getting Help on the MOO

The help system on MOOs is quite extensive. It's a good idea for you and your students to spend some time getting familiar with the MOO help indexes. A few minutes spent looking at the help system will save lots of time when actually interacting with others on the MOO. When you first type **help**, the MOO retrieves an index system similar to that shown in Figure 7.4.

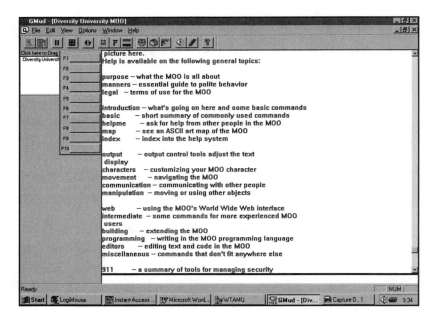

Fig. 7.4   The MOO Help system.

To get into the help system, you merely type **help *<topic>***. So, for example, if I wanted help on talking in a MOO, I would type **help communication**. The screen shown in Figure 7.5 appears.

As you can see, a list of all communication commands appear. To get help on a specific command, you again type **help *<topic>***. Thus, to get further information on the say command, I would type **help say**. The information shown in Figure 7.6 appears.

A class assignment designed to help students learn about the MOO help system is provided in MOO Assignment 7.5: "Getting Help on a MOO."

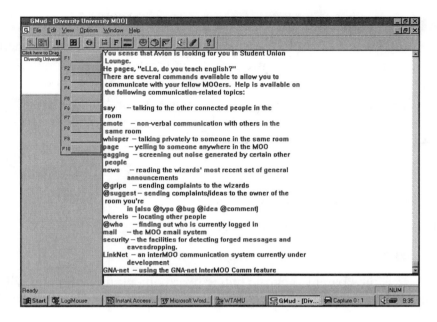

Fig. 7.5 The "Help Communication" menu.

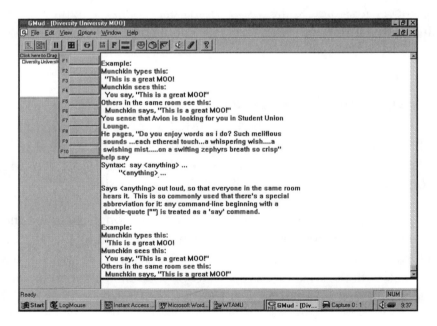

Fig. 7.6 Output of "Help Say."

Creating Objects on a MOO

Because of the way MOOs are structured, when you want to create something for your classroom, you need to use a command that tells the computer that you want a "thing object," such as a seat, called "whateveryouwant." So, for example, if I wanted to create a note board to use on the MOO, I would type

> **@create #16592 named "mynotes"**

where

> **@create** is the MOO command verb,
>
> **#16592** is the generic object number, and
>
> **"mynotes"** is what I want to call my notice board

The **#16592** is the "parent" generic notice board object; the computer will assign the "child" **"mynotes"** an object number of its own.

Creating objects is really quite simple once you start. Don't forget, however, that all objects are stored in the MOO database, so keep the number of created objects to a minimum. As always, if in doubt, ask the MOO wizards for help.

Creating Your Classroom

Because many teachers are starting to use MOOs as educational spaces, some MOOs have set up a generic classroom with many features in which to hold your classes. These generic classrooms make the job of creating your MOO classroom much easier than it was when I first started using MOOs.

Once you're somewhat familiar with the basic MOO commands, you should be able to build, stock, and use your virtual classroom within a week or two. The following discussion again makes use of the Diversity University MOO server; check with the wizards on the MOO of your choice about the options available there.

Setting Up the Classroom

Once you've created the room in which to hold your class, you can set it up as your classroom. If you created the room using the Generic Enhanced Classroom, #7208, you can start to add furniture. If you set up the room using a different generic, simply change the "parent" of the room to that of the Generic Enhanced Classroom by typing

chparent here to #7208

The capabilities of the enhanced classroom are extensive. Table 7.2 shows the commands available for the classroom and their descriptions.

Table 7.2   Commands for the Enhanced Classroom

Command	*Description*
@addfurn/@rmfurn <*object*>	Add/remove a piece of describable furniture
@authorize/@unauth Ken	Add/remove Ken from list of authorized users
cleanb	Erase entire blackboard
door open/closed	Restrict entry to persons in *current* class
@fix	Correct seating mixups if they occur
@mkclass/@rmclass Math	Add "Math" to list of classes taught here
register/unregister Ken	Add/remove Ken from *current* class
@restrictions on/off	Restrict special verbs to authorized users
@setup Math	Makes "Math" the *current* class

continues

Table 7.2   Continued

Command	Description
@stifle on/off	Restrict talking and emoting to those seated at small tables
@tutorial	View a short tutorial on using classroom
@who	Retrieves a list of logged-on users

In order to use all the features of the classroom, you need to *setup* the classroom for your classes and *register* your students. These are accomplished by using the commands @setup classroom and @register. For detailed instructions, type **help @setup** and **help @register**.

Education Tools on a MOO

Once you've set up your classroom, there are a number of educational tools available to use on a MOO. These tools simplify the tasks of preparing and displaying lectures, providing instructions and/or tests to students, and recording classroom sessions. While the instructions provided here are sufficient to create and use the tools, you should look at the detailed help available on the MOO and talk to other teachers and the wizards.

Lecturing on a MOO

Lecturing on a MOO is almost as easy as preparing and delivering a lecture in a traditional classroom. However, having said this, you need to know that MOOspace isn't really very conducive to lecturing. MOOs are active spaces; students can't be expected to "sit still and be quiet." To have them do so is to undercut the potential of MOOs as learning spaces. MOOs are uniquely designed to allow students the opportunity to create their learning spaces and to reflect upon that process.

Still, there are times that it's desirable to deliver course content material in a lecture format at the MOO. There are two tools designed to provide that capability—the slide projector and the enhanced lecture.

The Slide Projector

The slide projector (analogous to an overhead projector) is one of the most useful tools on a MOO, allowing you to input lines of text (22) to display to students in a room. The generic slide projector comes with a short slide tutorial explaining how to create and project your slides. To create your slide projector, type

@create #1650 named myprojector

The Generic Enhanced Lecture

The Enhanced Lecture is similar to the slide projector but allows far more flexibility in input and display capabilities. Lectures can be divided up into "sections" for logical breaks and to fit time constraints. To create your lecture tool, type

@create #16759 named mylecture

The Enhanced Lecture also comes with detailed instructions on how to operate it. There are some 26 help topics (tutor topics) that describe how to set up your lecture, enter text to your lecture, and display your lecture.

Tip for Success MOOs have their own text-editing capabilities, and you can certainly use them for creating material for your slide projector or enhanced lecture. However, these editors are rather primitive line editors and are thus not particularly user-friendly. If you are running under a Windows or Mac platform, you probably would prefer to create your lectures in a standard word processor and paste the text into the MOO. A short tutorial on MOO text editors (@notedit) is found in the text that follows.

Providing Course Material on a MOO

One of my favorite things to do on a MOO is to store and provide course content material for students. Students can visit the classroom at their convenience and review lecture material, notes, additional course readings not in the textbook, and take makeup tests.

In fact, once students become familiar with the MOO and working in a virtual environment, I almost stop lecturing in class altogether. Students are assigned readings on the MOO along with the textbook. Thus, they have my lecture notes available to them as they read their text.

I can save a lot of valuable class time in this fashion. Instead of orally delivering the lecture during class, students will have read it before class. Part of their reading assignment is to develop questions they have about the topic to bring to class. Thus, I can devote much more class time to questions and answers, discussion, and small-group activities.

The Generic Chaptered Book

The chaptered book is basically a collection of written notes that can be indexed or listed in a table of contents. It is similar to the MOO notice board but allows you more flexibility with note lengths and display. For example, the notice board is a good place to put up assignments or general help information for students. Notes are simply listed in the order they were written. With the chaptered book, however, you can place entire units online, broken up into "chapters" that are arranged sequentially in the order you determine. To create your own chaptered book, type

@create #1709 named mybook

The Bookshelf

As the name suggests, the bookshelf is an object designed to hold books. The advantage of using a bookshelf to store your reading materials is that it keeps track of the books you've placed on it. For example, if you place a book on the shelf named "topics," and the next time you "look" at the bookshelf it's not there, you can see who's taken the book. You can then contact the student to recall the book. To create your own bookshelf, type

@create #10936 named mybookshelf

To register a book on the bookshelf, type

@register *<bookname>* on *<mybookshelf>*

To place a book on the shelf without registering it, simply type

place *<bookname>* on *<bookshelf>*

Students can then type

take *<bookname>* from *<bookshelf>*

to read one of the books.

The Copyright Key

I had originally created the bookshelf in my MOO classroom to house additional readings not contained in our anthology. Then I realized that by putting up material on the MOO, potentially anyone could have access to the material. Panicking, I was ready to forget about the bookshelf and spend countless hours scanning and preparing copies to e-mail to my students. I realized, however, that even that might not get me out of the copyright bind.

The MOO wizards came to my aid and created a "copyright key." Using this key, I could encode the material so that it was unreadable by anyone who wasn't registered with the key. All I needed to do was to "register" my students with the key, a fairly simple operation taking up little time. To create your own copyright key, type

@create #7419 named *<key>*

and then register your students by typing

@add *<names in list format>* to key

Making Assignments on a MOO

MOOs are convenient for storing directions for assignments you've made. I often create assignments and put them up at the MOO for students to review. My students know that they need to check in at the MOO at least once a week to see whether there are any new assignments. The following two MOO tools—the Notice Board and the Classroom Black Board—were created to facilitate interclass communication.

The Notice Board

This education tool was designed to post short notices that people could easily retrieve on a MOO. When you post a message to the notice board, a short heading descriptor of the note is created with it. Thus, when students "look" at the notice board, they will see a numeric list of short titles. They can then "read" the notices by choosing one of the numbers. Along with assignments, you can post notices with "help" on using MOO tools in an assignment.

In my classroom, for example, I posted notices reminding students to tape their sessions, along with a short explanation of how to operate the tape recorder. To create your own notice board, type

@create #5266 named *<mynoticeboard>*

The Blackboard

All classrooms come equipped with a blackboard so there's no need to create one with @create. These blackboards are easy to use, just type

writeb *<text>*

Blackboards come in handy for students to leave you messages when they are at the MOO. Students can see the blackboard by typing **look blackboard**.

Taking Tests on a MOO

You can actually have students take tests or quizzes on a MOO. I don't worry much about cheating on quizzes—my students know that I'm more interested in their finding the information than in memorizing it. Also, much depends on the kind of quiz or exam you design whether or not taking it on the MOO is worth your while. Many of my quizzes are "active," asking students to use the Web slate or the gopher slate to find information that is the answer to the quiz question. Often, I'll put reading quizzes up at the MOO as well.

One great benefit is that I don't need to take up class time with these routine quiz activities; students can perform these tasks on their own at the MOO. For major exams, however, you'll probably still want to have students take them in your classroom under supervision.

Two objects exist on the MOO which can be used for taking tests—the Generic Survey Object and the Generic Customizable Object Creator. These are explained in the following sections.

The Generic Survey Object

The generic survey allows you to enter lines of text as "questions." It can contain single or multiline questions, and records the person's answer to each question. It will only accept one line responses so it works best for multiple choice or short answer tests.

To create your survey test, type

> **@create #759 named** *<mytest>*

The Generic Customizable Object Creator (GCOC)

This tool is more flexible than the survey object, but requires a bit more MOO know-how as a result. Actually, it is a generic object *creator* as indicated in the name, and a test is simply one of many possible objects. Moreover, the way it is currently set up, the creator will generate an object number for the finished product, thereby using up building quota (the number of objects you are allowed to build on the MOO). With a test, however, you can set it up so that the finished product (the answers) are e-mailed to you and the student, a choice that does not result in the assignment of an object number.

Extensive help is available for the object creator, and its uses are as varied as your imagination. One teacher, for example, has set up a pottery wheel that creates objects of the user's choice.

To create your own object creator, type

> **@create #20814 named** *<my creator>*

Keeping a Record

One of the tremendous benefits of teaching in MOOspace is that you can "log" or record class sessions or student-group sessions. These logs can be made available to students after the class, either by e-mail or file sharing. I use class logs throughout the semester. The object of their learning thus becomes the students' own experiences. Moreover, you can review the logs to see who is participating and who is not, to intervene in groups that are having problems, or to simply keep abreast of student interactions. Two MOO tools exist for logging sessions—the tape recorder and video camera; however, if you are using a MOO client such as TinyFugue, there is generally a logging function built into it. If you are not present at the MOO session, however, you will need to teach your students how to turn the tape recorder on and off.

The Generic Tape Recorder, Video Camera, and Tapes

The generic tape recorder is much simpler to set up and teach students to use than the video camera. Both tools, however, are basically set up to use a "tape" on which to record the session. Thus, you need to create both the recorder *and* the tape. You will also need to tell the recorder what tape to "use" to record the session. Thus, to create and use your tape or video recorder, you will need to type

> **@create #2978 named** *<myrecorder>*
>
> **@create #9 named** *<mytape>*
>
> **use** *<myrecorder>* **with** *<mytape>*

MOOs Plus the World Wide Web Equals WOOs

Technology is advancing so quickly, it is genuinely difficult to keep up. As recent as MOO technology is, it is nonetheless undergoing rapid development through integration with the World Wide Web. These new animals are called WOOs (Web, Object-Oriented). With a Java-enabled browser such as Netscape, you can visit and interact on a MOO via the World Wide Web. Figures 7.7 and 7.8 illustrate how this new technology looks and works.

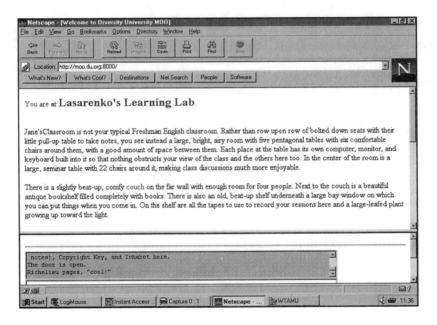

Fig. 7.7　An integrated Web and telnet environment.

The technology is moving rapidly. Currently, you can set the Web browser to embed a VRML view. Pretty soon, I can imagine being able to include video and audio files as well. Figure 7.8 illustrates the WOO environment with a VRML view.

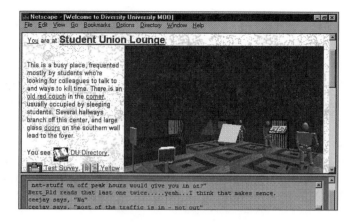

Fig. 7.8 Web environment with a VRML view embedded.

Teaching Students to MOO

The following assignments are designed to help familiarize your students with a MOO and to show them how to interact effectively in one. Students seem to respond quite enthusiastically to MOOspace, catching on very quickly. Soon, many of your students will be far more proficient at interacting in this environment than you or I.

MOO Assignment 7.1: Learning to Navigate

Subject: All

Grade: 7-12

Description: Students participate in an online scavenger hunt that requires them to use all the basic MOO commands for movement ("walk") and for picking up and returning objects to their proper places ("take" and "put" or "place").

Objective: To provide students the basic skills necessary to navigate on a MOO; to help students develop more sophisticated problem-solving skills.

Preparation: The MOO "Scavenger Hunt" is a feature object (FO) that you can add to yourself. Make sure you have your students type **@addfeature #15400** before starting. Also, give your students a handout of a map of

Diversity University and the commands for talking ("say") and paging ("page <person>") so they can ask for help if they need it.

Procedure:

1. After meeting your students in your classroom or at the DU Student Union, introduce them to the scavenger hunt. It's really pretty simple—a matter of typing **clue** to get the first clue to solve.

2. Tell your students to return to the Student Union or your classroom after a set period of time.

3. Your students should return to the MOO as often as necessary to solve the riddle or until you decide they've learned enough.

4. Have your students discuss in groups or as a class their answers to the clues or any problems they may have encountered and how they went about solving it.

Variations: I often require my students to write a paper about the experience after the small-group discussion.

Tip for Success There is nothing easy about this scavenger hunt. Be prepared for student frustration if they cannot locate a room or solve a clue. Make sure to remind them frequently that the point of the hunt is to learn about DU and how to navigate there.

MOO Assignment 7.2: Online Class Discussion

Subject: All

Grade: 7-12

Description: Students meet together online to "talk" about course content material.

Objective: To provide students an opportunity to become comfortable "talking" with others online; to help students master course content.

Procedure:

1. Create logon identities for your students.

2. Divide them into small groups if you want.

3. Have them meet at Diversity University and "sit" at tables or chairs in your classroom.

4. Have students record their conversations in their small groups.

5. Have students e-mail themselves the log of their conversation.

6. Ask students to examine their logs for key statements, issues of debate, decisions reached as a homework assignment.

7. Discuss the logs with students in the next class period.

MOO Assignment 7.3: Online Peer Review

Subject: All

Grade: 7-12

Description: Students meet online to review one another's papers, laboratory reports, or solutions to problems outside of class.

Objective: To help students improve the quality of their work by one-on-one tutoring and peer review.

Procedure:

1. Have students arrange to meet with one another in their groups at a pre-arranged time.

2. Make sure students have e-mailed one another copies of their work *before* the meeting.

3. Have students sit together at a table to discuss their work.

4. Make sure students are told to create a log of their conversations.

5. Students should provide help to one another on their written assignments.

6. Students should e-mail themselves the log of the conversation.

Tip for Success Depending on the age range of your students and the amount of practice they've had working with one another, you might want to provide a list of detailed questions they need to address when reviewing one another's work.

MOO Assignment 7.4: Creating Your Character

Subject: English, Social Studies

Grade: 7-12

Description: Students are asked to adopt the names of cartoon characters on the MOO. They then describe their cartoon characters and spend some time interacting on the MOO. Students are asked to guess the real identities of their classmates.

Objective: To help students grasp the concept of ethos in their writing; to help students understand the dynamics of character, identity, and communication.

Preparation: At some MOOs, particularly if you're going to want your students to use their real names later in the semester, you'll need to contact a MOO wizard for help setting up this special exercise. Later in the semester, you'll need to have your students create another character with their real names. Also, pair students up or divide them into groups of three for this exercise. Otherwise, it becomes too unwieldy for a short class assignment.

Procedure:

1. Assign each student a random cartoon character name.

2. When students log onto the MOO, have each of them **@describe** themselves without revealing too much about themselves. Make sure each student knows that their description must be true, must correspond as closely as possible to their "real" selves.

3. Students should meet and interact with one another for a period of several weeks.

4. Students should keep detailed notes or a diary of their responses, ideas, and attitudes toward the others on the MOO.

5. Using the information obtained from **look** *<character>* and the log of their MOO interactions, students should try to "guess" who their class-mates are.

6. Have students write up an analysis of their problem-solving, addressing:

   a. How they initially reacted to the character based on the cartoon name.

   b. How the character's description influenced the way they began to interact with that character.

   c. What verbal "clues" helped them determine the identity of their classmate.

   d. What steps they took to try to determine the character's "real identity."

MOO Assignment 7.5: Getting Help on a MOO

Subject: All

Grade: 7-12

Description: Students are asked to find out all they can about a particular or group of related MOO commands and to share that information with their classmates.

Objective: To help students become familiar with the MOO help system; to provide students the opportunity to produce and share knowledge with their classmates.

Procedure:

1. Divide students into small groups.

2. Assign each group a MOO command or group of related MOO commands.

3. Students should look in the MOO help system to find the help entries on that command or group of commands.

4. Students should share the information they find with their classmates.

↯ Tip for Success I usually like to have students produce a hand-out, flyer, or brochure covering the information they found and telling the other students *where* the information can be found. For younger students, you might want to have them present the information orally to their classmates.

Moo Projects

The following projects are designed to help your students work on a MOO both with students from the class and with others far away. Any of the projects can be modified to accommodate your students' levels of expertise.

MOO Project 7.1: Working with the World

Subject: All

Grade: 7-12

Description: Students collaborate with a class from another part of the country or world on a paper or project.

Objective: To involve students with course content, to improve their ability to work with others from disparate geographic and/or socioeconomic backgrounds, and to help students master course content more effectively through working with others.

Preparation: Contact and discuss possible projects with a teacher from another part of the country or world. Prepare assignment handouts that detail your expectations and procedures for students to follow.

Procedure:

1. Divide your students into small groups and pair them with a small group from the collaborating class.

2. Provide some class time for your students to meet with their groups from the other class on the MOO to get to know one another and to

brainstorm on the paper or project. Make sure students exchange e-mail addresses.

3. Determine a schedule during which your students can meet during or outside of class with their groups on the MOO to discuss ongoing drafts or work in progress.

4. On a prearranged schedule, students should e-mail drafts of the paper to one another and meet on the MOO to discuss those drafts. If you have them collaborate on a project, make sure everyone knows what portion of the project s/he is responsible for.

5. Groups should share their work with the class as a whole when the paper or project is completed.

MOO Project 7.2: Double Jeopardy

Subject: All

Grade: 7-12

Description: Students both create and play a kind of jeopardy game.

Objective: To help students master course content material.

Procedure:

1. Divide the class into two groups. One group will construct the game; the other will play it.

2. Have group 1 construct a jeopardy game based upon terms, concepts, and definitions you want to have students master.

3. Group 2 should "play" the game until every student has provided all or nearly all the correct answers.

4. Later in the semester or year, do this project again, switching groups.

Tip for Success Make sure you talk to the MOO wizards about this project before beginning. If your students are young, you probably will have to supervise their building more closely than if they are more capable of working independently. If none of your students are able to build on the MOO (some MOOs prohibit students from building), you can construct the "game" based on questions and answers provided to you by the game-building group.

Figures 7.9 and 7.10 show a variation of this project, designed by "Doppler" at Diversity University MOO.

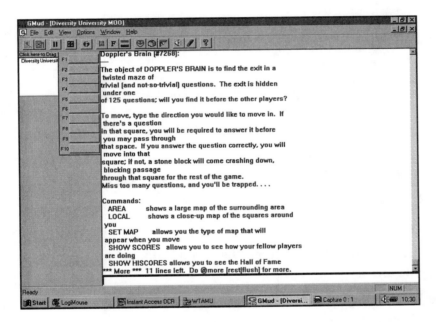

Fig. 7.9 Doppler's "The Brain" project at Diversity University MOO gives students a chance to exhibit their knowledge.

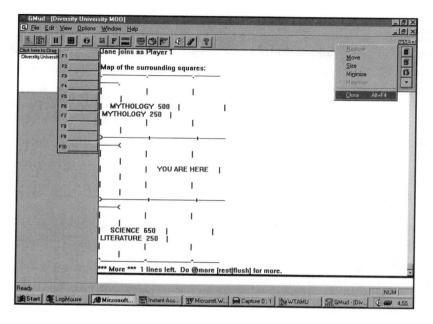

Fig. 7.10 Question map inside Doppler's "Brain."

MOO Project 7.3: Hysterical Recreations

Subject: Social Studies

Grade: 7-12

Description: Students create rooms based on historical time periods or geographic areas.

Objective: To help students master course content concepts and material; to help students integrate course content material.

Procedure:

1. Divide students into small groups.

2. Have students plan on paper or in logged MOO sessions what objects they will need to include, the description of those objects, and any other information that they will need to think about in advance.

3. Students should then create those objects on the MOO.

Tip for Success You might want to extend this project over several years, having one class build on the start made by the previous class. Maybe you need to determine how much time you can have students realistically devote to the project.

MOO Project 7.4: Literary Losers

Subject: English, Social Studies

Grade: 7-12

Description: Students create rooms and objects that pertain to a literary work they are studying.

Objective: To help students better understand the concept of literary analysis; to help students understand the components of literature; to help students understand the relationship between literary works and the cultures that produce them.

Procedure:

1. Divide students into small groups.

2. Have students write and exchange information about the material they need to include, or distribute a handout specifying what information you want students to include.

3. Have students meet on the MOO to create and describe those objects.

Tip for Success Again, consider dividing up this project over several terms, classes, or years. I generally have students work on small segments of the overall project in any given semester, primarily due to time constraints. Building MOO rooms is labor- and time-intensive, and I can generally only provide about four weeks for students to accomplish their tasks. Also, having a class build on and continue a previous class's work helps build a sense of community that is broader than just their own class. Slowly but surely a sense of a large and ever-growing community of Lasarenko Project learners is arising throughout the Texas Panhandle.

Figures 7.11 and 7.12 show a sample of a literary project built by two of Leslie Harris's sophomore literature survey classes at Susquehanna University.

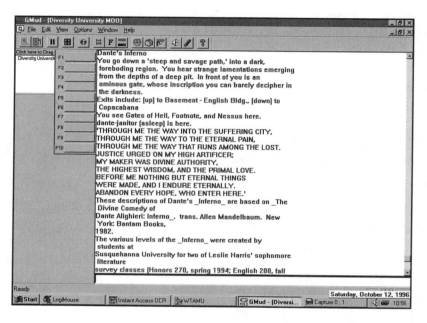

Fig. 7.11 Dante's *Inferno*.

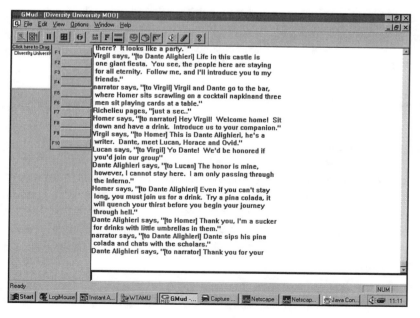

Fig. 7.12 An Infernal Conversation at the Inferno.

MOO Project 7.5: SIMulation City

Subject: All

Grade: 7-12

Description: Students create rooms based on course content such as rain forests, small ecosystems, or set designs for plays.

Objective: To help students master course content concepts and material; to help students integrate course content material.

Procedure:

1. Divide students into small groups.

2. Have students collaborate and exchange in writing the text descriptions for objects they want to include.

3. Have students create the objects on the MOO.

Figure 7.13 shows the first room of a rain forest simulation.

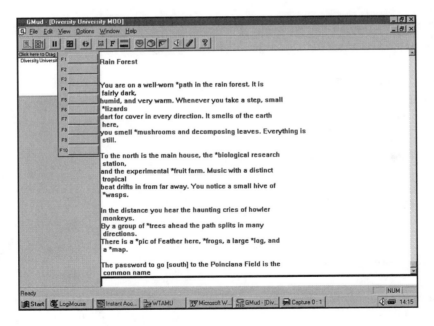

Fig. 7.13 The Rain Forest at Diversity University MOO.

Extending Your Repertoire

Much of the information you would want about MOOs can be found on the World Wide Web. One of the most extensive sites of current research on MOOs and MUDs is Lucien Sims' page at

http://lucien.sims.berkeley.edu/moo.html

Another excellent source is a special issue on MOOs in *Kairos*, an electronic journal, located at

http://english.ttu.edu/kairos/1.2/index.html

Bartle, Richard. "Interactive Multi-User Computer Games."
http://lucien.sims.berkeley.edu/mudreport.ps

Bruckman, Amy. "Gender Swapping on the Internet."
http://lucien.sims.berkeley.edu/gender-swapping.ps
Also available from **ftp://ftp.parc.xerox.com**

_____. "Programming for Fun: MUDs as a Context for Collaborative Learning." **http://lucien.sims.berkeley.edu/necc94.ps**

Cherny, Lynn. "Gender Differences in Text-Based Virtual Reality." **ftp://ftp.parc.xerox.com/pub/MOO**

Curtis, Pavel. "Mudding: Social Phenomena in Text-Based Virtual Realities." **ftp://ftp.parc.xerox.com/pub/MOO**

Curtis, Pavel and David A. Nichols. "Muds Grow Up: Social Virtual Reality in the Real World." **ftp://ftp.parc.xerox.com/pub/MOO**

Fanderclai, Tari. "Muds in Education: New Environments, New Pedagogies." **http://sensemedia.net/sprawl/16880**

McDonough, Jerome. "Being There: The Use of Cyberspace in Computer-Mediated Communication." **http://lucien.sims.berkeley.edu/cyberspace.ps**

Moock, Colin. "Communication in the Virtual Classroom." **http://arts.uwaterloo.ca/~camoock/virtual_classroom.htm**

Sempsey, James. "The Psycho-Social Aspects of Multi-User Dimensions in Cyberspace: A Review of the Literature." **http://www.netaxs.com/~jamesiii/mud.htm**

Sims, Lucien. The MOO Command Quick Reference **http://lucien.sims.berkeley.edu/MOO/quick-reference.txt**

Towell, John and Elizabeth Towell. "Internet Conferencing with Networked Virtual Environments." (first appeared in Internet Research). **http://www.mcs.anl.gov/home/towell/IntRes.html**

Looking Both Ways

As we have seen, MOO technology is a terrific tool for extending active learning strategies in and out of the classroom. Students have the opportunity to become actively engaged in "real-world" simulations and experiences that ask them to *use* the course material in problem-solving, not simply to memorize and spew it back to us. Another excellent resource for teaching that is growing by leaps and bounds is the World Wide Web. The Web is a rapidly expanding arena of information, an interactive learning environment, and a forum for student publishing, as you'll see in the next chapter.

And Then Came the Web and It Was Good

Everyone's talking about it and everyone's excited about it. Growing so fast that even now 10,000 more people are connecting to it. In two short years, it's gone from a relatively unknown medium to TV's and the newspaper's new "hot" topic. Practically every large company in the U.S. has those funny little initials that appear at the bottom of your TV screen. It's the World Wide Web.

The World Wide Web (WWW) is often used synonymously with "the Internet." In fact, the WWW is the largest-growing portion of the Internet and is used far more than the other aspects we've looked at earlier in the book. One way of thinking about the World Wide Web ("Web," for short) is that it is a graphical version of gopher and ftp. In fact, the Web has gopher and ftp capabilities built right into it. Because of its graphical nature, the Web thus allows text retrieval and video, audio, animation, and graphic capabilities. Put all those together on one Web "page" and you have a powerful tool for learning. In a sense, the Web is like a giant multimedia CD-ROM that doesn't require any special hardware.

Multimedia Helps Learning

As we've previously discussed, multimedia enables student learning to the extent that it can target different learning styles. The benefit of the Web is apparent in this regard. One of the advantages of the Web over CD-ROM learning tools is that you get to create the learning environment. I know I've often been frustrated with the educational CD-ROMs available from education software publishers; often, it's too limited or based on a heuristic I don't care for. With the World Wide Web, however, I can create my own—or students can create their own—multimedia presentations, lectures, and Web sites.

Learning 24 Hours a Day

Another of the many advantages to using the World Wide Web for learning is its unrestricted access. Most public libraries have a Web-capable browser and many students are getting Web browsers for their home computers. In addition, many businesses are springing up that provide safe environments for students to use computers that are directly connected to the Internet at very reasonable costs, many as low as $4 an hour. 24-hour-a-day access means 24-hour-a-day learning.

Often, in restaurants, grocery stores, or waiting on long lines, I hear people talking about this new thing called the Internet. Generally, given the recent media "take" on the subject, their comments are negative. "I sure hope our schools aren't going to allow our kids to have access to that terrible thing" is a refrain I often hear. Frightened by the recent hype over recipes for bombs and pornographic material, these people judge the Internet unfairly, few taking the time to investigate it on their own. Certainly this information is available on the Web—assuming you have an incredible number of hours to search for it. Moreover, this information is even more readily available elsewhere in printed form. As always, it's a question of knowing where to look for it.

Denying students access to the Internet is not the answer; educating them to its more positive uses is. I'm rather a crusader in this regard; I don't think there's any information that should be censored. Abuse is an inescapable corollary of good use. I'd far prefer my students spending time surfing the Net for pornographic material than watching the latest greatest violence fest that passes for entertainment in our society. Moreover, while surfing the Net there's a good chance they might come across some useful information that will sidetrack them from their original search.

TECH TALK Surfing:
Spending time on the World Wide Web just seeing where it takes you; synonymous with "cruising."

Research Can Be Fun

It never ceases to amaze me just how curious kids are when left to their own devices. If I assign them a research topic, I get moans, groans, and hostile looks abound. If instead I ask them to choose a topic that interests them and report back to the class on what they found, they won't stop looking. I've even had students who had the audacity to tell me they weren't quite ready to give their reports—there were just one or two more sites they needed to check out!

While their interest is obviously somewhat due to the excitement of a new medium, much of it is due to the nature of the Web as well. Students have greater control over the direction and content of their searches. WWW Assignment 8.1: Surf City details how to start your students off using the Web.

I teach at a small, regional university with a relatively poor library system. They do the best they can with limited funds; however, there is not much printed information available to students and faculty. The World Wide Web has been a tremendous aid to my research, putting me in touch with other faculty interested in the topic, with listserv archives, with Web sites on the topic (complete with downloadable articles), and with library catalogs.

OCLC has its search services online, and I can search the major indexes and journals for articles and books in my field from home. Information search and retrieval services is just now coming into its heyday. Education and government organizations are joining together to investigate ways to organize and deliver the flood of information available through the World Wide Web. In the not too far distant future, a global information system will start to take shape. What an exciting time and project to be alive and engaged in!

The World Wide Web May Be Addicting

According to national polls, reports are starting to come in that document the latest threat to our nation's youth: the World Wide Web. Students have been known to surf this new medium on an average of three hours a day. The general public has voiced concern over this new wave of student inactivity, fearing that such extensive use of computer technology may be habit-forming and lead to greater addictions.

Other segments of the population are worried that this surfing activity may be linked to cancer. Scientists are analyzing the data available, and while hesitant to voice any conclusions based on short-term studies, are generally agreed that such use is definitely not carcinogenic.

On the contrary, major national health spokespersons state that moderate long-term use of the Web seems to increase synaptic response, thus contributing to increased memory capabilities and critical thinking skills.

Syllawebs Replace the Syllabus

One of the greatest advantages of the World Wide Web is its improved delivery capability for course materials. Students no longer have any excuse for not doing homework, reading text material, or pleading ignorance of assignment due dates. I put a copy of my course syllabus up on the World Wide Web (see Figure 8.1), thus saving paper copy costs, although I do urge my students to print out a copy of the syllaweb if they don't have a home computer.

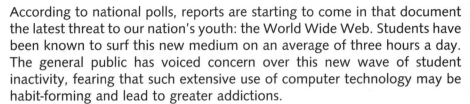 **Syllaweb:**
Online adaptation of the traditional course syllabus. Synonymous with "silly-webs."

Tip for Success Many students are still relatively computer-illiterate. I generally print out a copy of the tentative assignment schedule to distribute on the first day of class. In addition, I distribute hardcopy instructions on how to access the course syllaweb.

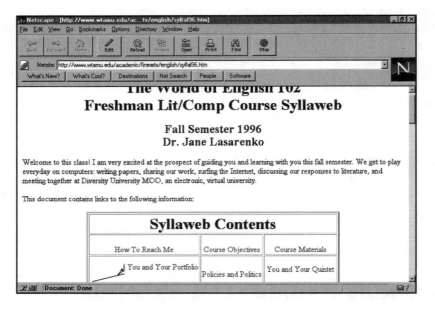

Fig. 8.1   A typical syllaweb.

Another advantage of putting your course syllabus online is the capability to link to other sites of interest to students. I generally create a course home page that contains links to online OWLs for grammar and writing help, to search engines, and to outstanding course-related Web sites.

TECH TALK Home Page:
The first page of a Web site; a personal page published on the World Wide Web.

Figure 8.2 shows a typical course home page.

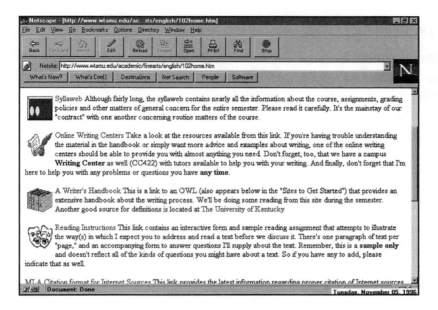

Fig. 8.2 English 102 home page.

"Webtures" Replace Lectures

Another advantage to using the World Wide Web in teaching is the capability to display your lecture material with links to related information. My students often think literature exists in a vacuum, totally unrelated to anything else going on in society and the culture. Of course, they "know" that literature must be a reflection of a culture, but when it comes right down to it, they seem to forget that fact when dealing with literary works. Using the Web in my teaching really helps them remember that fact.

When teaching Kate Chopin's *The Awakening*, for example, I use the Web extensively. Students are unfamiliar with the historical, social, and cultural milieu of the turn-of-the-century Creole population. To help them better understand the story, I might create—or have them create—a Web study guide that contains links to information about that era. We create links to Web sites dealing with music, art, Creole culture, feminism, and other American literature. Web Project 8.2: Time Capsules details how to accomplish this type of activity.

Improving Reading Skills

The Web can be used for a number of exercise-type activities to help students master course content. My students often come into my freshman literature and composition classes with relatively poor reading and analytical skills. I use the interactive capabilities of the Web to help them learn to slow down their reading and to grasp better the conventions of literary analysis.

Figure 8.3 shows a sample page of my reading activity. I broke up Chopin's short story, "The Story of an Hour," into small textual chunks of about 2-3 sentences each. I then highlighted words in the story that were important to an appreciation of Chopin's intentions in the story. Each page had an area for students to write their comments and responses to my questions. As the story progressed, I asked students to develop their own set of "important words" or to explain how my highlighted words were important. At the bottom of each page was a button that, when clicked, would send a copy of the students' responses to me and to the students.

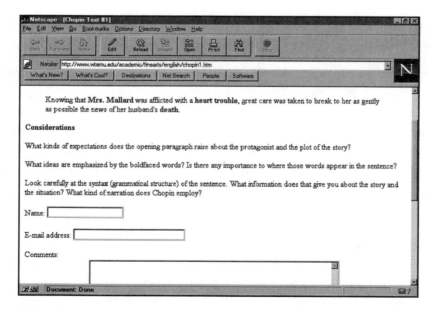

Fig. 8.3   Typical Web page with form input capability.

Interactivity versus Interaction: Hypermail and Hypernews Improve Class Listservs/Newsgroups

The interactivity provided by form input improves the efficacy and community-building properties of newsgroups and listservs. Hypermail (and Hypernews for newsgroups) is a Web-based interface for mailing lists. The programs take the "raw posts" and thread them by author, subject, and date. It also groups the posts into primary posts and their responses, as well as by replies to responses. Thus, with hypermail you can get an overview of the structure of the conversation.

You can set up a hypermail page that contains a field for comments and replies that will get sent to the list directly from the Web page. Students can browse the list and choose which posts to reply to. This interactivity speeds up the electronic conferencing of e-mail lists, providing a more immediate feel to the ongoing conversation.

Class journaling can be more easily managed with hypermail as well. Students need not go to a mail program to first view the posts, need not wait as long before they get a sense of the ongoing conversation, and can respond more quickly and easily. You can design the form to send the comments directly to the list, to the sender, and to yourself as well. Alternatively, you can design the form to send the comments to another page, designed to capture only the comments to the original posts.

Real Audiences for Real People

We all know that students write much better when they have a "real" purpose and a "real" audience. Somehow, writing for the teacher isn't "real" to them—it's a game designed to get a grade, not a purposeful action in the real world designed to achieve something. That it is just as "real" in a classroom setting is a difficult concept for them; consequently, their writing often reflects their ambivalence (often hostility) toward the assignments.

When writing using the Web, however, students know that their writing will be read by many people, not by just the teacher. For most students, this public audience is a real incentive to improve their writing skills. They may not care about appearing careless to their teacher, but let the public have access to their work, and students proofread very carefully.

Student Publishing Arrives

The advent of the Web is starting to change our concept of publishing, both what it means to "publish" and the form of those publications. For the present, "bandwidth" is limitless, and students have the opportunity to see their work displayed along with that of other young scholars.

TECH TALK **Bandwidth:**
The amount of data a telephone line or fiber cable can handle.

This opportunity will probably be limited in the future as more and more of the world's population start to use and produce information for the Internet. It behooves us to use this opportunity as much as possible while we have it.

At present, I comment on student papers right on the Web. I create a link from part of their text to another document that contains my responses to their text. By doing so, I need not "mark up" their papers with my marginal writing; their text remains their text.

In addition, I'm creating a "grammar file" of hypertextual links to OWL help files. Thus, if a student has a grammatical error in their paper, rather than simply pointing it out, I can direct the student to the germane grammar help directly. I know from experience that when I mark a grammatical or typographical error on a student's paper, she rarely goes to a handbook to find out how to correct the problem. By linking to online help, however, the student has the help file right there.

I also plan to have a space on each student's paper page that allows others to respond to the student's work directly. The respondent's text appears as a hypertext link off the student's paper and is e-mailed directly to the student as well. By providing this capability, students can experience the nature of scholarly work at a young age, and see their work as part of an ongoing conversation among peers.

Students can also perceive and participate in the kinds of changes that are taking place in online scholarly work. As a result of publishing on the Internet, I know my attitude toward my work has changed dramatically. I no longer think of my work as solely mine, immutable, and fixed forever. I now think of my work as snapshots of thought at a particular time; my "text" is subject to the wisdom and input of other minds at work, changing with the responses and ideas of those others. My concept of "text" is now one that is fluid, mutable, plural, and many-voiced.

Navigating the Web

Graphical User Interfaces (GUIs) make navigating the World Wide Web as easy as pointing and clicking with your mouse. There are search engines on the Web as well that make finding information a little easier. To date, these search engines are still rather crude; using them is like finding yourself in a black hole of information. A search on "education," for example, is likely to yield over 100,000 hits. More sophisticated searching tools are currently under development; soon, they will in all likelihood far exceed their printed counterparts.

While navigating the Web is as easy as pointing and clicking with your mouse, there is nonetheless some rationale behind the way Web documents are referenced and accessed that you and your students need to know.

Web Terminology

While the Web is fairly easy to navigate, there are still some terms with which you and your students need to be familiar. Since the Web is a very large collection of hypertext documents located on computers around the world, the Web pioneers developed a system to identify every document and file accessible on it.

This nomenclature assigned a uniform resource locator (URL) to every file according to the following paradigm. First comes the Internet protocol, "http" (hypertext transfer protocol) followed by a colon (http:). Next come two forward slashes to separate the protocol from the rest of the address: http://.

The remainder of the address is formatted in a similar fashion to e-mail addresses (see Chapter 3). Immediately after the protocol is generally "www," signifying the World Wide Web. Then comes the domain name of the computer on which the document resides, followed by the path location of the file on that computer. For example, the URL of my freshman class syllabus is

http://www.wtamu.edu/academic/finearts/english/102home.htm

Netscape and other browsers now allow other protocols when connecting to remote computers. Thus, to access a gopher file at my university through the World Wide Web, you would start the address with **gopher://gopher. wtamu.edu**; to download a file through an ftp site, you would start with **ftp:// ftp.wtamu.edu**.

Searching for Documents on the Web

As mentioned earlier in the chapter, information retrieval on the Web is at best a process of trial and error, at worst a frustrating experience for students. The available search tools are still in their infancy, generally based on "key-words" that are identified in the HTML documents themselves.

There are a number of commercial search tools currently available through your browser's home page: Yahoo!, Infoseek, Lycos, Web-Crawler, and Magellan are the largest and best known.

Each of these search tools is based on a Boolean "and" search logic. Thus, if you search for information on Jane Austen, you will get a listing of every document on the Web containing the word "Jane" and "Austen." This result can be quite daunting and frustrating at times. If you want to retrieve documents based on a Boolean "or" strategy, you need to type your search words in with quotation marks, as in "Jane Austen."

Nonetheless, be prepared for huge numbers of hits when doing a Web search. Tell your students not to be daunted by the enormous amount of information they might need to sift through to find information. Tell them, also, that much of what they find initially might be quite useless for their purposes; that they should start off by trying to simply enjoy the experience of "surfing the Net."

As more and more students and academics are starting to publish material on the Web, some genuinely useful Web sites have developed. In the humanities, for example, Alan Liu of Berkeley created a huge humanities Web site that now serves the world called "The Voice of the Shuttle" (see Figure 8.4). If my students are working on any humanities-related project, I tell them to start their search from there rather than from one of the commercial search tools.

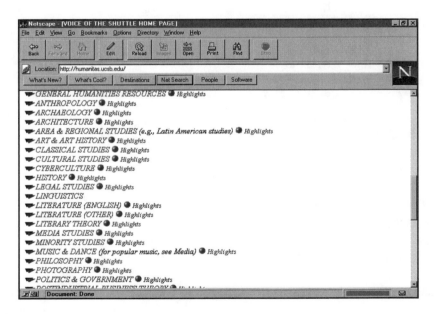

Fig. 8.4 The "Voice of the Shuttle" home page.

The URL for the "Voice of the Shuttle" page is

http://humanitas.ucsb.edu/

An excellent starting place for the Sciences is "Infomine" (see Figure 8.5), located at

http://lib-www.ucr.edu/physci/

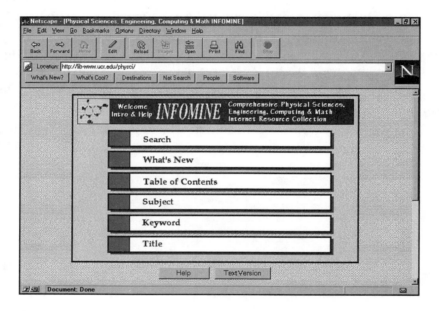

Fig. 8.5 Searching for science-related information.

A recent addition to research starting points is "Purely Academic" (see Figure 8.6), developed by Alan Spencer and located at

http://apollo.maths.tcd.ie/PA/

Because of the wealth of information available on the World Wide Web, it's relatively easy to get "lost" among myriad links. It's a good idea to have your students get into the habit of marking locations they find useful by creating a *bookmark* for that page (see Figure 8.7). With a bookmark, you can return to that location quickly, simply by pointing and clicking.

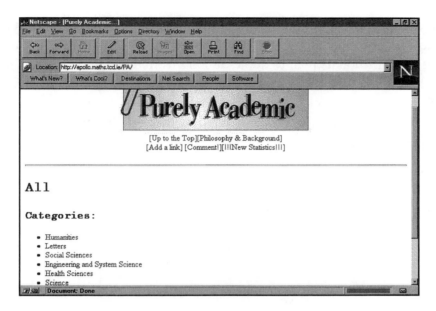

Fig. 8.6 The "Purely Academic" home page.

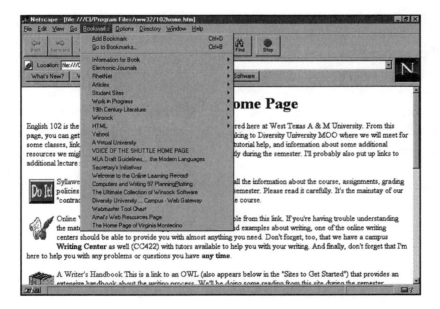

Fig. 8.7 Creating a bookmark in Netscape.

Another time-saving technique when doing research is to have students save the most helpful files they find to their disks. Saving files to disk is particularly useful if students plan to quote directly from the material on the Web, but cannot link to the exact location of the material on the Web page. Saving a Web page to your own disk is very simple; you simply click File, Save As in the File menu (see Figure 8.8). A window then comes up asking where you want to save the file.

Fig. 8.8 Saving a Web page in Netscape.

Another technique useful in classes with only one or two computers is to have students print out the Web pages they find. In my own classroom, I tend to discourage printing out Web pages; every student has his or her own computer workstation, and printing out many Web pages can be very time-consuming and costly. But if students don't have easy access to computers, printing out the pages may be the best alternative.

To print out a Web page, you simply click the printer icon or "File, Print" (see Figure 8.9).

Fig. 8.9 Printing a Web page.

Learning to Create Web Pages: HTML

HyperText Markup Language (HTML) is the code used to create documents for the World Wide Web. HTML is really quite simple to learn; three or four codes are all you need to know to create a basic Web document. You can create a Web document in any DOS-based text editor or your favorite word processing programming. A Web document is simply a plain ASCII text document saved with the file extension .htm or .html. The most important thing to remember is *to save the file in plain DOS text*, and not in WordPerfect (*.wpd) or Word (*.doc) or Works (*.wks) format.

HTML is primarily made up of a series of toggle codes; you first turn on the code and then you must turn it off. Thus, a basic Web document is composed of the following:

<html>

<head>

</head>

<body>

</body>

</html>

That's all there is to a basic document for the World Wide Web! All HTML documents are composed of two main parts or "containers:" a heading container that holds all the information about the document—its title, author, and related information—and a body container that holds all the text and associated multimedia files that you want to display.

Notice that all HTML codes must appear in angle brackets (< >). Web browsers are designed to read anything contained in the < >'s as codes. Thus, the initial <html> tells the browser to "begin reading the following text as designed for the World Wide Web." The final </html> tells the browser "turn off the beginning html code," signals that "this is the end of the document."

The same idea is true for the <body> tags above. The first one tells the browser that the contents of the document between the two tags is the "body" of the document. The first one turns it on, the second turns it off. Notice that / is used to toggle off all HTML codes.

Most other HTML codes are used for formatting the text, with two exceptions: the tags for making a hypertext link and for inserting an image or sound file. The codes for these two actions are <a href> and <img src>.

The Anchor Hypertext Reference Code (a href)

The anchor (<a>) code is used for a variety of purposes, the main one being to create a hypertext link to another document on the World Wide Web. To accomplish the link, you merely modify the anchor code "a" with a *hypertext reference code* and provide the name of the file you want to link to as follows:

> <a href="http://www.wtamu.edu/academic/finearts/english/
> ↪sylfal96.htm"> Syllabus </a>

In the preceding example, I have instructed the browser to link to the specified file (always put in quotation marks) when someone clicks the "Syllabus." The browser will read all text between the initial anchor reference and the </a>, the code for toggling off the anchor code.

If you want to link to a file on the same server as your HTML document, it *must* be located in the same directory as the HTML file. For example, on my course home page, I have links to several other files related to the course. All those files are located in the same directory as the home page. In the 102 home page, one of those links, Course Policies, is coded as

       \<a href="policies.htm">Course Policies\</a>

Another link, Grades, is coded as

       \<a href="grades.htm">Grades\</a>

Thus, the only time I need to enter the full path name to the file is when it is located on a remote server.

The Image Source Code (\<img src>)

This code is used to include images, sound files, pictures, icons, and video clips into your Web document. There are only a few image file types that browsers can display at present. The most common image file format for the Web is .gif format. Most Web browsers will also easily display images saved in .jpg (or .jpeg) format.

Not all programs provide the capability of saving images in one of these two formats; WordPerfect images, for example, are stored in .wpg format. You will probably need a graphic conversion program such as GIFConverter, for the Macintosh, or LView Pro, for the PC, if you are going to get into Web publishing on a grand scale. These programs are easily downloaded from the World Wide Web itself.

As with the anchor code, you must provide the file name of the image in quotation marks as follows:

       \<img src="filename.gif">

Other Basic HTML Codes

While unnecessary for "bare-bones" Web documents, the following codes help to add some "spice" to your first Web pages. Moreover, some of the basic codes given here and previously can be modified with additional "arguments" to format the appearance of the text in your document.

The Paragraph Code (<P>)

The paragraph code, as the name suggests, is used to break up your text into paragraphs. In the latest version of HTML (Wilbur or HTM 3.2), you can actually specify how you want the paragraph formatted. Let's say you wanted to align your paragraph flush right; you would do so by typing

<P align=right>Type your text here. </P>

The Heading Code (<H>)

As again implied in the name, the heading code is used to offset your title text in a larger type font than the rest of the text. Headings come in six sizes, 1 to 6. H1 represents the largest text size possible, h2 is somewhat smaller, and so on down to h6. To create a large page heading, you simply type your text between <h1> and </h1> as follows:

<h1>This is my home page</h1>

The List Code (<UL>)

There are several kinds of lists possible in HTML, but the one you'll probably use most frequently is the unordered list (<ul>). The other two kinds of lists are the ordered list (<ol>) and the definition list (<dt>). The primary difference among the lists is the way they are formatted on the browser screen. The ordered list has numbers preceding the text and the definition list has a one-line definition term followed by several indented lines of definition. The unordered list is preceded by bullets.

To create an unordered list, you type in the list code <ul> first. Then you need to identify each item of the list using the list code <li>, short for list item. For example, if you wanted to create a short list of items needed for your course, you would create an unordered list as follows:

<ul>

<li> The text book

<li> A 3-ring notebook

<li> Three 3-1/2 inch computer disks

</ul>

You can even specify the kind of bullet (round, square, filled) you want to use in your lists. For example, you can make all bullets in the list square by modifying the initial <ul> code to read <ul type=square>.

The Body Tag Attributes <body>

As we saw earlier, all HTML documents are composed of two main parts: the heading information and the body information. The <body> tag can be modified with arguments that control the color of the background, the text, and the links you create. All colors used in Web documents are based on a hexadecimal code, ranging from "FFFFFF" (the strongest red, green, blue [RGB] combination) to "000000" (the weakest red, green, blue combination). Because white is the strongest combination of all colors, it is represented by the code FFFFFF; black, as the absence of all color, or the weakest combination, is 000000. All other colors are coded on this basis—a combination of red, green, and blue. You can easily download a complete list of all the colors and their codes from the World Wide Web by doing a search from Yahoo! or Infoseek on "HTML colors."

When putting together a Web document, all the information about the colors of the background, text, and links are contained in the <body> tag. Thus, if you want to create a page with a black background with white text and red links, you would type

<body bgcolor="#000000" text="#FFFFFF" link="#FF0000">

where, "bgcolor" stands for background color, "text" for text, and "link" for the links.

Notice, too, that you must put the color reference in quotation marks and include the number sign, #.

Putting It All Together

Let's try now to create our first document for the World Wide Web. Open up a new document in your favorite word processor. For this example, I'll open up a new document in Word, but remember that it really doesn't matter; WordPerfect or Write or simply NotePad will work just as well.

The first thing to do is create the HTML backbone, the heading portion and the body portion. Your file should now look like the first example shown earlier:

```
<html>
<head>
</head>
<body>
</body>
</html>
```

Now, let's insert some information about the document in the heading container—the title of your HTML document, "homepage.htm." The page should now read:

```
<html>
<head>
<title>Home Page
</title>
</head>
```

```
<body>
</body>
</html>
```

Good. Now let's put something on our home page. First, we need to decide what we want the document to look like in terms of background colors and text colors and so on. Remember that all that information goes into the body tag. Let's make the background of our page blue, the text, white, and the links we create, red. Your HTML document should now look like

```
<html>
<head>
<title>Home Page
</title>
</head>
<body bgcolor="#0000FF" text="#FFFFFF" link="#FF0000">
</body>
</html>
```

Now to add some text to the page. I'm going to make "home page" and my name a level-1 and level-2 header, respectively. Your page should now look like

```
<html>
<head>
<title>Home Page
</title>
</head>
<body bgcolor="#0000FF" text="#FFFFFF" link="#FF0000">
<center>
```

```
<h1>Home  Page</h1>
<h2>Dr. Jane Lasarenko</h2>
</center>
</body>
</html>
```

Notice I was really sneaky and put in another code—a center code. I decided that I wanted those two lines centered on the screen. To do that, I need to tell the browser to center the lines between the center on and center off (<center> and </center> codes. Go back now and insert those two codes for your own document.

Now I'm going to go back and add some text and links to my document. I'm sure you'll want to add information different from mine, but for now, give some basic information about yourself and use the link I provide to my course syllabus. That way you can check later to make sure it works. Your document should look something like the following:

```
<html>
<head>
<title>Home Page
</title>
</head>
<body bgcolor="#0000FF" text="#FFFFFF" link="#FF0000">
<center>
<h1>Home Page</h1>
<h2>Dr. Jane Lasarenko</h2>
</center>
<p align=left>Hello and welcome to Dr. Lasarenko's Home Page
for the World Wide Web. I'm a professor at West Texas A & M
```

University and have been using the Internet to teach my first-year composition courses for the last four years. The new technology allows for some exciting changes in the classroom. Please take a look at my

<a href="http://www.wtamu.edu/academic/finearts/english/ 102home.htm"> course syllabus

</a> to see some of the ways technology can enhance your teaching.

</body>

</html>

Now it's time to save your document and take a look at what you've created in Netscape or whatever browser you use at your school. First, save your document in plain text format, (ASCII [DOS] text option in WordPerfect, MS-DOS text in Word), and provide the file extension .htm, as shown in Figure 8.10.

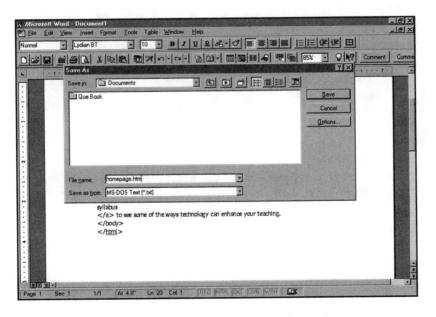

Fig. 8.10 Creating an HTML file for the World Wide Web.

Notice that I named the file to correspond to the information given in the <title> tag, "homepage.htm." Close your word processor and open Netscape or your favorite browser. Choose, "File, Open File in Browser," highlight your homepage.htm file, and click OK. You should now see the home page you just created; it should look something like the one shown in Figure 8.11.

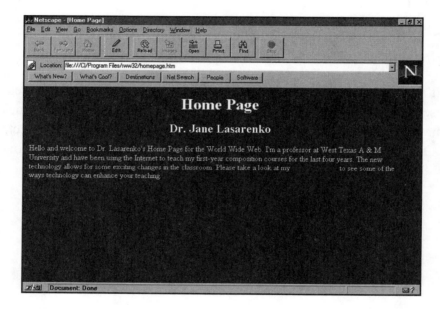

Fig. 8.11   Viewing your new home page in Netscape.

If you're connected to the Internet, try clicking the "course syllabus" link. You should see my English 102 Home Page in a few moments.

Congratulations on creating your very first document for the World Wide Web!

Teaching Students to "Web"

The following assignments are designed to teach students the basics of HTML and World Wide Web navigation.

WWW Assignment 8.1:
Surf City

Subject: All

Grade-level: All

Description: Students "surf the Net" to present a collection of interesting Web sites to their classmates. This exercise works well as a prelude to WWW Assignment 8.3: Critiquing Web Sites.

Objective: To provide students the basic tools for navigating the World Wide Web.

Procedure:

1. Divide students into groups and have each group determine a subject of interest to them all.

2. Students should begin their search from one of the commercial search engines, so make sure your browsers are preset to a starting point. (Alternatively, provide students with an Internet address.)

3. Have students create bookmarks for all the sites that pertain to their topic. Make sure they also save one or two of the better sites to their disk or to the hard drive.

4. Have students discuss the sites and choose five "best sites" about their topic.

5. Have the groups report their findings to the rest of the class, either by a presentation using the World Wide Web, orally, or in a written format such as a brochure.

Tip for Success I often assign my students topics that deal with the World Wide Web for this exercise. For example, I might have one group find sites that provide html backgrounds, icons, and images; another group might work on general introductions to html coding. Another variation that works well as a prelude to WWW Assignment 8.3: Critiquing Web Sites is to assign the same topic to all student groups.

The most important thing to keep in mind is to make these initial forays onto the World Wide Web as fulfilling for the students as possible. I strongly recommend presetting your browser to a good search engine. Students have a great deal of difficulty typing URLs accurately at first and get very frustrated after repeated failures. Maximize the success potential of this assignment.

WWW Assignment 8.2:
Information War

Subject: Science

Grade-level: All

Description: Students go on an "information hunt" to get the answer to a course-related question. The "winners" are the first group to find the answer to the question.

Objective: To provide students with a basic familiarity with Web searches.

Procedure:

1. Divide students into small groups.

2. Distribute a handout with the specific question to all groups. In this example, give all students the question "how long would the resulting line be if you laid out all the blood vessels in an adult human body?"

3. Have students start from a commercial search engine site such as Netscape or Yahoo!.

4. Have students keep a record of their search strategies for later discussion.

5. Make sure you have a prize available for the "winners."

Tip for Success While this assignment works well for all grade levels, you probably want to leave the topic fairly broad for younger students and the information to be found fairly general. The older the class, the more specific your questions can and should be.

The answer to the question assigned in this exercise can be found off the Franklin Institute Science Museum page:

http://sln.fi.edu/biosci/biosci.html

WWW Assignment 8.3:
Critiquing Web Sites

Subject: All

Grade-level: 7-12

Description: This assignment builds on the results of WWW Assignment 8.1: Surf City by asking students to create formal reports that justify their choices of good Web Sites.

Objective: To help students develop critical thinking and evaluation skills.

Procedure:

1. Divide students into small groups (or ask them to meet with the same group as they worked with in WWW Assignment 8.1).

2. Have students address the following question: Discuss and define your criteria for a "good" Web Site. Think about what things led you to choose the site you did as "the best."

3. Have the class meet and each group share their criteria with everyone in the class. Develop a class set of "Web Site Criteria."

4. Have students meet with their groups again and discuss the attributes of the site they chose according to the "Web Site Criteria" developed in step 3.

5. Have students prepare a written report of their evaluation.

Helping Students Generate Criteria

Be prepared to guide and help your students generate these criteria, especially the younger students. Older students are generally capable of developing these criteria fairly independently; younger students need more help verbalizing their criteria. For younger students you might consider distributing a handout listing the following criteria if they fail to do so themselves:

- Overall Design

  Effective use of visual rhetoric—color, text, layout on the screen, graphics

  Ease of information access—effective use of headers and lists

- Content

  Usefulness of information presented

  Usefulness of links

  Information given appropriate to the audience and purpose for the site

- Purpose

  Clear, identifiable purpose to the site

  Clear, identifiable audience for the site

WWW Assignment 8.4:
HTM What?

Subject: All

Grade-level: 4-12

Description: Students learn the basics of HTML by comparing the codes with those of their favorite (and familiar) word processor.

Objective: To help students learn the basics of HTML.

Preparation: Prepare a handout with some basic HTML codes: <p>, <b>, < i >, <H1> <center>, <body>, and any others you feel are critical to your students' needs.

Procedure:

1. Divide students into groups of two to three if you have enough computers available.

2. Have students open up a short document in their favorite word processor.

3. Ask students to turn on View, Reveal Codes (or the analogous view in your school's word processing program).

4. Have students format the document in several ways—centering the title, putting some words into boldface, some into italics, and justifying the text left and right.

5. Have students make a list of the codes that appear when they format the document.

6. Distribute a handout of basic HTML codes.

7. Ask students to compare the two lists and match the respective codes; <b> with bold, for example.

8. Have students discuss the similarities and differences between the HTML codes and the word processing codes.

Tip for Success This exercise generally reassures students that HTML is not difficult or mysterious. For younger students, who may not be familiar with word processing codes, you might revise this exercise to ask them to find definitions from the Internet for basic HTML codes. As you long as you preset your browsers to a good introduction to HTML, students of all ages should have little difficulty. You might consider having students prepare handouts for the rest of the class on different aspects of HTML coding; one group investigating and preparing a handout on tables, for example, another one on lists, and so on.

Projects for the World Wide Web

The following projects are designed to get you started with student projects for the World Wide Web and are primarily intended to spark your imagination. No "cookbook" for student projects could ever be written—you are limited only by your imagination and your class's enthusiasm.

WWW Project 8.1:
Home Page Madness

Subject: All

Grade-level: All

Description: Students create and critique their own home pages on the Web.

Objective: To help students master the basics of HTML coding; to help students understand basic concepts of visual rhetoric.

Procedure:

1. Explain the project carefully to your students, making sure they understand the requirements you expect for their successful home page completion. Depending on the grade level of your students, you may or may not require them to include links to other places or graphics files, for example.

2. Tell each student to bring two computer disks to class with them on the day(s) you plan to work on this project.

3. Have each student search the Web for backgrounds, colors, graphics files, and so on, that they want to include on their page. Make sure they understand the rules for using others' images and files on their pages. I generally require my students to send a copy of a response to a request for permission to me directly, whether or not the information is in the public domain. It's better to be safe than to break the emerging copyright law.

4. Each student should write the code for his or her home page and e-mail the file to another student for review.

5. When all students have successfully prepared their HTML file, you will need to load it on the school's Web site (unless your school provides Internet file space for students).

6. Have students critique at least one other student's home page according to preestablished criteria.

Tip for Success You will probably have to provide a fair amount of help in this project to younger students. One approach I have found works fairly well is to link this project with a unit on ethos, the writer's character on paper. I tell my students that they should design their home page to showcase their personality. You might want to tell your students to create their home page to say something about themselves as Americans in a social studies class, or something about their ethnic backgrounds in a multicultural unit. Needless to say, I also make this an ungraded assignment.

WWW Project 8.2:
Time Capsules

Subject: All

Grade-level: 7-12

Description: In this project, students put together miniature "time capsules" or "snapshots." The time period can be as broad or narrow as fits your course objectives. One group, for example, has put together a time capsule on the battle of Gettysburg, another on the ancient world (see Figure 8.12).

Objective: To help students integrate course content with other subjects; to develop higher order critical thinking skills.

Procedure:

1. Divide students into small learning groups, designating at least one group as "project editors."

2. Distribute a handout to all students indicating the names of their group mates, the topic assigned to their group, the topics assigned to all other groups, a list of the responsibilities of each group, and a few starting points for their investigation.

3. Have students start gathering material about their topic or preparing a written plan of their portion of the project.

4. Have students discuss their research at every stage of the project in their groups and with the class as a whole.

5. Have students submit their research to the project editors for review and revision suggestions.

6. Have students create the Web site.

Tip for Success This project is very labor-intensive. You might consider designing the project to last for a number of years, each class building on and expanding the work of the previous years. Alternatively, consider collaborating with another class; if you live in the South, find a class from somewhere above the Mason-Dixon line with which to work on the project. Another possibility is to join one of many emerging education technology corporation projects that are designed to bring schools together for projects such as this one. (See Appendix C for a list of education resources on the World Wide Web.)

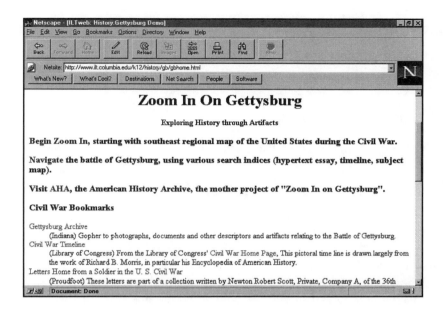

Fig. 8.12   The "Zoom In On Gettysburg" project home page.

WWW Project 8.3:
Topic Webs

Subject: All

Grade-level: K-5

Description: This project involves your students in learning about particular topics in your curriculum, for example, dinosaurs. Students create material for a Web site on the topic, including stories, poems, songs, pictures, and written descriptions. Two examples of this project can be found at

http://www.geocities.com/SunsetStrip/2028/index.html

and

http://squire.cmi.k12.il.us/hcs/dinosaur/index.html

Objective: To help students better understand specific course content topics.

Pictures of this project's home pages are in Figures 8.13 and 8.14.

Procedure:

1. Explain the project to students.

2. Ask students to create their pictures, poems, stories, and written descriptions of the dinosaurs.

3. Scan student input into separate files.

4. Put together the Web site.

Tip for Success This project can be very time-consuming for the teacher, especially if you're not very comfortable creating Web documents already. Make sure you have some help lined up for this one.

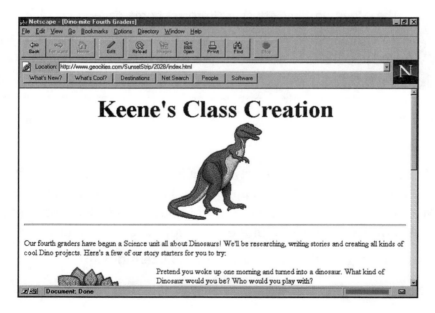

Fig. 8.13 Keene's Class Creation.

Fig. 8.14 Holy Cross's "Dino-mania" home page.

Extending Your Repertoire

Butler, Brian. "Using WWW/Mosaic to Support Classroom-Based Education: An Experience Report." *Interpersonal Computing and Technology Journal* 3.1 (1995): 17-52.

Caverly, David C.; Broderick, Bill. "Techtalk: World Wide Web and Developmental Education." *Journal of Developmental Education* 19.2 (1995): 36-37.

Davis, Philip. "Welcome to the World-Wide Web." *Computers in Libraries* 15.1 (Jan 1995): 51-55.

Dyrli, Odvard Egil. "Surfing the World Wide Web to Education Hot-Spots." *Technology & Learning* 16.2 (Oct 1995): 44-46,48,50-51.

LaRoe, R. John. "Connecting Classrooms to the Web: An Introduction to HTML." *Association of Small Computer Users in Education (ASCUE) Summer Conference. Proceedings* (28th, North Myrtle Beach, South Carolina, June 18-22, 1995).

Lindroth, Linda K. "Internet Connections." *Teaching PreK-8* 26 .4 (Jan 1996): 78-79.

Machovec, George S., Ed. "Electronic Journals: Trends in World Wide Web (WWW) Internet Access." *Online Libraries and Microcomputers* 14.4 (Apr 1996): 1-6.

Neal, Nancy L. "Research and Publication on the World Wide Web: A Fifth Grade Class' Experience." (1995): Eric No: ED384345.

Peraya, Daniel. "Distance Education and the WWW." *Education at a Distance* 9.7 (Jul 1995): 20-23.

Wei He, Peter; Knapp, Sara D. "Electronic Reserve with WWW: A Promising Way to Enhance Classroom Instruction." *Journal of Educational Technology Systems* 24.2 (1995-96): 119-25.

Glossary of Terms

Acceptable Use Policy (AUP)   A policy that states the conditions that apply to Internet use. These policies define the rules concerning abusive language, illegal acts, and inappropriate information access. For example, many school districts prohibit the use of state-owned equipment for accessing porno-graphic material or for sending mail containing abusive language.

Alias   Shortened form for **Al**so **i**dentified **as**. Used as a synonym for your login name.

Archie   A search engine for ftp site files.

Article   A message posted to a USENET news group or a listserv mail list. Synonymous with *post*.

ASCII   American Standard Code for Information Interchange. ASCII text format is an unformatted text code. As a result, it is easily transferable from one word processing program to another or from e-mail or USENET posts to a word processor.

Asynchronous   Time-delayed or time-deferred computer mediated commu-nication. E-mail is a form of asynchronous communication, as are USENET posts.

Bandwidth   The amount of data a modem or fiber optic cable can transfer in a given time.

BBS   **B**ulletin **B**oard **S**ystem. An electronic software program that allows users to hold discussions and exchange files.

Binhex   Shortened form of **BIN**ary **HEX**adecimal. Binhex can convert executable files into ASCII format or a form capable of being e-mailed. To use a file that has been "binhexed," you need to "unbinhex" it after you download it to your computer.

Bit   **B**inary dig**it**. The smallest unit of computer data. Bits combine to form bytes when transferring information.

Bitnet   **B**ecause **it**'s **t**ime **net**work. Bitnet is perhaps the original academic network system. Most institutions have changed now to the Internet's academic domain, .edu.

Bookmark   A place marker of a site in gopherspace or on the World Wide Web. By making a bookmark, you can easily return to that location.

Browser   A program that allows you to access or explore the Internet, particularly the World Wide Web. Mosaic and Netscape are examples of World Wide Web browsers.

Bps   **B**its **p**er **s**econd. The higher your modem's bps, the faster your data will travel.

Byte   8-10 bits. A complete unit of computer data—words, for example. One character on the screen is a byte.

Chat   A kind of electronic discussion. See *IRC* (Internet Relay Chat).

Chatroom   The cyberspace location of an electronic discussion or conference using chat software.

Client program   Software that allows users to find and access information on the Internet. A *browser* is one kind of Internet client; *gopher* or *ftp* are others.

CMC   **C**omputer **M**ediated **C**ommunication. Software programs and tools used to communicate with others via computer.

Compress   A method of reducing a file's size for faster transmission. Files on the Internet are generally compressed in .zip format. In order to use the file, you must decompress it first using a program such as pkzip or winzip.

Connect time   The amount of time you are physically connected to the Internet or a database located on the Internet.

Cyberspace   First coined by William Gibson in his science fiction classic, *Neuromancer*, cyberspace refers to the virtual worlds on the Internet. These worlds can be virtual communities, such as MOOs and MUDs and IRC chatrooms, but can also refer to local networks.

Dial-Up Connection   An Internet connection made through a host computer or through an Internet Service Provider (ISP).

Direct Connection   A permanent Internet connection, usually established through a T1 cable. Direct Internet connections are generally much faster than a dial-up connection.

DNS   **D**omain **N**ame **S**ystem. The current system used to identify computers directly connected to the Internet. All computers on the Internet are identified by a numeric IP address; most computers have a word name also associated with it. Common domain endings are .edu (educational institutions), .gov (government institutions), .com (commercial entities), .org (nonprofit organizations), and .net (Internet service providers).

Download   To retrieve a file from a remote computer to your own.

Electronic conferences   A synonym for listserv or USENET discussions. See also *Mailing List.*

Elm   A UNIX-based, free e-mail program.

E-mail   Electronic mail. Messages sent from a person at one computer to another person at another computer or location.

Emoticon   Also called "Smiley." A visual, typographic depiction of an emotional state. For example, :).

E-pal   An e-mail pen pal.

Eudora   A very popular e-mail program.

FAQs   **F**requently **A**sked **Q**uestions. Questions that are commonly asked about Internet-related topics and sites.

Fetch   An ftp command to retrieve (download) files from the Internet. Also a Macintosh program for ftp.

FidoNet   A global network bulletin board system for K-12 newsgroups.

Flame   An insulting, acrimonious, and inflammatory e-mail message.

Flame War   An ongoing verbal exchange of flames. See also Flame.

Freeware   Free software that can be retrieved from the Internet.

Ftp   **F**ile **T**ransfer **P**rotocol. A method for downloading or uploading files from one computer to another via the Internet.

Gopher   A program to find and obtain files on the Internet. Gopher works via a text-based menu system that links information from many universities and gopher servers.

Home page   The first page of a Web site. Many people with Internet access have created their own "home page;" in this meaning, the term refers to a document that contains information about the individual.

Host   A computer that is directly connected to the Internet.

HTML   **H**yper**T**ext **M**arkup **L**anguage. The language that creates and formats hypertext documents to be displayed on the World Wide Web or intranet.

HTTP   **H**yper**T**ext **T**ransfer **P**rotocol. The method by which computers communicate to display World Wide Web pages.

Hypertext   Text usually identified by another color, underlining, or boldfacing that contains links to other documents or locations, graphics files, sound files, and movie clips. Files created for the World Wide Web are in hypertext format.

Information superhighway   A synonym used for the Internet.

Internet   A group of computers linked together via a global network of fiber optic cable and telephone lines.

Internet Explorer   A graphic browser developed by Microsoft for the World Wide Web.

Intranet   A group of computers linked together via a network that may or may not be directly connected to the Internet.

IP   Internet Protocol. The language that structures the way information is transmitted across the Internet.

IP Address   A four-part number (separated by "." [dots]) used to identify an Internet host computer.

IRC   Internet Relay Chat. A large chat network on the Internet. To chat, you must have chat-specific software that is designed to link to an IRC server. Users can join together in a "chatroom" or on a "channel" and talk to one another in "real time" (synchronous communication).

ISP   Internet Service Provider. A company that provides people access to the Internet and e-mail. ISP companies usually charge a fee for this service in addition to "connect time" charges.

Kilobyte   Unit of measurement equal to 1,024 bytes.

LAN   Local Area Network. A small group of computers, usually confined to one institution or building, linked together via ethernet cables.

Link   A portion of a Web page (a word, phrase, or graphic) that is coded to connect to a different location when activated by clicking it with a mouse.

List   See listserv and listproc.

Listproc   One of the two most common software programs for managing e-mail discussion lists. See also *listserv*.

Listserv   The other most common software program for managing e-mail lists. See also *listproc*. Also used as a synonym for electronic mail conferences and discussions.

Login   The process of identifying yourself to a computer; the name you use to identify yourself to a remote computer, as in "login name." This process almost always requires a password.

Lurk   To subscribe to an electronic mail list but not post any messages. Many lists have thousands of subscribers, but only a handful may actually participate in any given discussion. The nonparticipants are lurking on the discussion, taking the information posted by others but not contributing anything of their own.

Lynx   A text-only browser for the World Wide Web.

Mailing lists   Synonym for electronic conferences and listserv/USENET discussion lists. Participants communicate via e-mail messages, which are sent to everyone subscribed to the list.

Megabyte (MB or M)   1,000,000 bytes. Most computer hard drives are at least 1.6M.

Modem   **Mo**dulator, **DeM**odulator. A device that connects your computer to a telephone line, which in turn connects to another modem on a remote computer.

Moderator   A person in charge of an electronic conference. Often, listservs are moderated; messages sent to the list are screened by the moderator who decides which ones are appropriate to be posted to the entire list.

MOO   **M**UD, **O**bject-**O**riented. A MOO is a text-based, multi-user virtual environment.

Mosaic   The first graphical browser developed for the World Wide Web.

MUD   **M**ulti-**U**ser **D**imension or **D**ungeon. A text-based virtual environment, usually associated with games such as Dungeons and Dragons. Also used to refer to "MUSHes" (Multi-User Shared Hallucinations) and "MUSEs" (Multi-User Shared Environments).

Multimedia   Documents and programs that contain a variety of media such as sound, pictures, video clips, animation, and text.

Net   A popular abbreviation for the Internet.

Netscape Navigator   The most popular browser for the World Wide Web.

Network   Two or more computers linked together that can share files and information.

Newbie   A person who is new to an area of the Internet. Thus, while you may be quite accustomed to the World Wide Web or e-mail, you may still be a novice where it comes to chatting or mooing or listserv discussions.

Newsgroup   A USENET discussion group. Members send posts or articles on specific topics under discussion.

Newsreader   A program used to retrieve and read articles from newsgroups.

NNTP   Network News Transfer Protocol. The method by which USENET articles are transmitted.

Node   A computer connected to a network. "Node" is often used synonymously with "host."

Offline   Not connected to the Internet.

Online   Connected to the Internet or an Internet Service Provider.

Packet   A collection of about 1,500 bytes of data. Computers break up data bytes into packets for transmission across phone and fiber optic lines. Each packet is reassembled into complete information units when received by the remote computer.

Page   A document on the World Wide Web.

Password   A way to identify yourself to a computer or a network. Passwords should combine both letters and nonletters and be at least five characters long. Passwords protect you from someone else using your account. You are responsible for all computer activity generated under your login name and password, so take the time to choose a random combination of letters and characters for your password.

PC   **P**ersonal **C**omputer. A familiar way of referring to your desktop or laptop computer.

PINE   **P**rogram for **I**nternet **N**ews and **E**-mail. A UNIX-based popular mail program and USENET news program.

Post   An e-mail message or USENET article sent to a listserv or newsgroup.

Port   A method for identifying some Internet applications on remote computers. For example, you might telnet to a remote computer by typing in the IP number; if you want to access the MOO on that computer, however, you need to include a port number at the end. Most MOOs use one of two port numbers—7777 or 8888. The address for Diversity University MOO is 128.18.101.106:8888 where 8888 is the port number. If you telnet just to 128.18.101.106, you'll be access for a login name and password to the remote computer—something you don't have.

PPP   **P**oint to **P**oint **P**rotocol. A method that allows your computer to connect to a host or Internet service provider via modem. This protocol allows your computer to make the TCP/IP connection necessary for your computer to be seen and recognized on the Internet.

Prompt   A character or group of characters that asks a user to enter information or commands.

Reply   An e-mail message or USENET article that is sent as a response to someone else's post or article.

Search engine   A computer program that allows you to locate documents and information on the Internet. There are numerous search engines available on the World Wide Web. The most popular are Yahoo!, Infoseek, and AltaVista.

Server   A computer that has been configured with software to allow it to run programs and make information available to other computers.

Shareware   Software you can download from the Internet to try it out for a specified period of time. Shareware should be registered with the author if you decide to keep it. Most shareware costs only a nominal fee.

Signal to noise ratio   A way of describing the ratio between the amount of information versus the amount of "junk mail" on a mailing list or USENET newsgroup. High signal to noise ratios indicate a great deal of junk on the list or site.

Signature   A file that is appended to the end of all your outgoing e-mail messages or USENET news articles. The file should contain (as should all your e-mail messages) at least your full name and e-mail address. Many people include their snail mail addresses, business phone numbers, and favorite quotes.

Site   An Internet host computer that allows remote access.

SLIP   Serial Line Internet Protocol. An older method for connecting computers to the Internet via a modem and telephone line. SLIP connections serve the same function as PPP connections but are not as reliable a method.

Snail mail   Mail sent via ground or air transport as opposed to e-mail.

Spam   An inappropriate message or, more generally, an advertisement sent to listserv mail lists or USENET newsgroups. Avoid sending spams or you'll be sure to get flamed.

Subscribe   The method of joining a listserv discussion list or USENET newsgroup.

Synchronous   "Real-time" electronic discussions that take place via the Internet. MOOs, Chatrooms, and network conferences are examples of synchronous communication.

TCP/IP   Transmission Control Protocol/Internet Protocol. The communication language(s) that allow computers on the Internet to "talk" to one another. You must have TCP/IP software or capability on your computer to access the Internet.

Telnet   A method (program) that allows you to connect to a remote computer and to use the software or information stored on that remote computer.

Thread   A series of e-mail posts or USENET newsgroup articles on a specific subject (usually identified in the subject line).

Timeout   The result of a failure by one computer to respond to another within a specified amount of time.

TN3270   A version of telnet that works with IBM mainframe computers.

Transfer mode   The method by which you set your computer to transfer files. You can send files in ASCII text mode or in binary (computer) mode.

URL   Uniform Resource Locator. A standardized method for recognizing the exact location of every document or site located on the World Wide Web. "Address" is often used synonymously with URL. For example, the URL of text documents all start with **http://**; to access a gopher site via the World Wide Web, you would start the URL with **gopher://**. To connect to an ftp site, you start the URL with **ftp://**. The remainder of the address is the IP number or domain name of the site to which you want to connect.

UNIX   A computer operating system. Most mainframes, servers, and hosts use UNIX for their operating system because it is much more flexible and complex than those we generally have on our PCs.

USENET   An international collection of over 10,000 newsgroup discussion lists. You must have a USENET newsreader to access these electronic conferences.

Veronica   Very Easy Rodent Oriented Netwide Index to Computerized Archives. A tool designed to locate information on gopher servers by keyword.

WAIS   Wide Area Information Search software. A tool that searches all Internet documents by your specified keyword(s). WAIS will also rank the search results.

WAN   Wide Area Network. Extends over a large geographical area.

Web An abbreviated and popular term for the World Wide Web.

WWW World Wide Web. The collection of all hypertext documents and their associated media available on the Internet. The term originated from the name of the UNIX program that was first designed to locate documents on other UNIX servers.

Academic Listservs and USENET Groups

The following information is abstracted from the *10th Revision Directory of Scholarly Electronic Conferences* by Diane K. Kovacs (**diane@kovacs.com**) and The Directory Team.

Listservs

The following academic listservs are meant to provide a starting point for your research into electronic communities. Please read Chapter 4 first if you are unfamiliar with electronic conferences.

General Education and Technology Listservs

AERA-C

Subscription Address: **listserv@asuvm.inre.asu.edu**
List Address: **AERA-C@asuvm.inre.asu.edu**
Moderator's Address: Gene V. Glass, **Glass@asu.edu**

Topic: Discussion for AERA Division C: Learning and Instruction. Sponsored by the American Educational Research Association (AERA) and the College of Education at Arizona State University.

AERA-K

Subscription Address: **listserv@asuvm.inre.asu.edu**
List Address: **AERA-K@asuvm.inre.asu.edu**
Moderator's Address: Gene V. Glass, **Glass@asu.edu**

Topic: Discussion for AERA Division K: Teaching and Teacher Education. Sponsored by the American Educational Research Association (AERA) and the College of Education at Arizona State University.

BEE-net

Subscription Address: **listserv@titan.sfasu.edu**
List Address: **BEE-net@titan.sfasu.edu**
Moderator's Address: Glenn Blalock, **gblalock@titan.sfasu.edu**,
and Thomas Philion, **philion@uic.edu**

Topic: Forum in which new elementary, middle school, and secondary
English teachers initiate conversations with peers across the country and
participate in the kinds of interactive, reflective discussions that contribute to
professional development. BEE-net and the soon-to-be-established BEE-net
Web site can help to connect and to expand the various learning communities
established in English education classrooms and programs across the country.

CBNVEE

Subscription Address: **listserv@MCMUSE.MC.MARICOPA**
List Address: **CBNVEE@MCMUSE.MC.MARICOPA**
Moderator's Address: Greg Swan, **swan@mcmuse.mc.maricopa.edu**

Topic: Networked virtual reality software such as MUSE, tinyMUSH, and
MOO.

CORELINK

Subscription Address: **listproc@mercury.cair.du.edu**
List Address: **CORELINK@mercury.cair.du.edu**
Moderator's Address: **craschke@du.edu**

Topic: Educational goals, outcomes, and "core curriculum." Subject matter
includes, but is not limited to, the consideration of courses, texts, syllabi,
lesson plans, new pedagogues and technologies, trends and initiatives within
the education reform movement, and the politics and policies surrounding
core curriculum. Discussion group and distribution list is open to K-12 and
post-secondary educators at the national and international level. CORELINK
is tied administratively to the gopher files of the American Association for
the Advancement of Core Curriculum.

COSNDISC

Subscription Address: **listserv@bitnic.educom.edu**
List Address: **COSNDISC@bitnic.educom.edu**
Moderator's Address: Ferdi Serim, **ferdi@cosn.org**

Topic: Consortium for School Networking Discussion Forum.

CTI-L

Subscription Address: **listserv@irlearn.ucd.ie**
List Address: **CTI-L@irlearn.ucd.ie**
Moderator's Address: Claron O'Reilly, **CLARON@irlearn.ucd.ie**

Topic: The use of computers in teaching.

EDTECH

Subscription Address: **listserv@MSU.EDU**
List Address: **EDTECH@MSU.EDU**
Moderator's Address: Edtech Moderator, **21765EDT@MSU.EDU**

Topic: Educational technology.

EDUTEL

Subscription Address: **listserv@vm.its.rpi.edu**
List Address: **EDUTEL@vm.its.rip.edu**
Moderator's Address: Comserve Staff, **edutel-request@vm.its.rpi.edu**

Topic: Computer-mediated communications (CMC) applications in educational contexts.

INFED-L

Subscription Address: **listserv@CCSUN.UNICAMP.BR**
List Address: **INFED-L@CCSUN.UNICAMP.BR**
Moderator's Address: Eduardo Chaves, **CHAVES@CCVAX.UNICAMP.BR**

Topic: The uses of computers (or what is usually called informatics) in education, broadly conceived. Contributions may deal with the various uses of computers in higher, secondary, elementary, or informal education. Discussion of the philosophical and sociological implications of computer-aided teaching and learning is also welcome.

Information Technology & Teacher Education (ITTE)

Subscription Address: **listserv@DEAKIN.OZ.AU**
List Address: **ITTE@DEAKIN.OZ.AU**
Moderator's Address: Chris Bigum

Topic: An e-conference for teacher educators interested in the new information technologies.

JEI-L

Subscription Address: **listserv@umdd.umd.edu**
List Address: **JEI-L@umdd.umd.edu**
Moderator's Address: Christopher Keane, **keane@earthsun.umd.edu**

Topic: The use of technology in the K-12 classroom, especially CD-ROM scientific data sets. This mailing list, maintained by the Joint Education Initiative, is meant to provide a medium through which educators and other interested parties can exchange information, learn of new developments, learn of new science and technology resources, and exchange technical concerns. Though the prime interest of the list centers around users of the USGS JEDI CD-ROM set, discussion of other uses of technology in the K-12 classroom are encouraged and welcomed. All subscribers will receive an ASCII version of the Joint Education Initiative newsletter through the list.

K12-EURO-TEACHERS

Subscription Address: **majordomo@lists.eunet.fi**
List Address: **k12-euro-teachers@lists.eunet.fi**
Moderator's Address: Louis Van Geel, **lvg@k12.be**

Topic: The exchange of information related to K-12 education/educators and the promotion of school-related data communications in Europe. The content complements the K-12 hierarchy of newsgroups (echomail) available through USENET and FidoNet. This mailing list is also distributed through FidoNet as an echomail conference. Thus, it will not be sent to subscribers in the fidonet.org domain. FidoNet users, please check with your regional echomail coordinator for the K12.EURO.TEACHERS conference or at any 2:nn/777 node in Europe. Keywords: Primary Education (European).

LRN-ED

Subscription Address: **LRN-ED-Request@listserv.syr.edu**
List Address: **LRN-ED@listserv.syr.edu**
Moderator's Address: Richard Burkett, **rburkett@minet.gov.mb.ca**, or Carolyn Sprague, **richlist@ericir.syr.edu**

Topic: Discussion for K-12 teachers.

MMEDIA-L

Subscription Address: **listserv@itesmvf1.rzs.itesm.mx**
List Address: **MMEDIA-L@itesmvf1.rzs.itesm.mx**
Moderator's Address: Alejandro Kurczyn S., **499229@itesmvf1.rzs.itesm.mx**

Topic: Discusses the use of multimedia in education and training.

MULT-ED

Subscription Address: **listproc@gmu.edu**
List Address: **MULT-ED@gmu.edu**
Moderator's Address: Jack Levy, **jlevy@gmu.edu**

Topic: Multicultural education; cosponsored by the National Association for Multicultural Education and George Mason University.

RPE-L

Subscription Address: **listserv@uhccvm.uhcc.hawaii.edu**
List Address: **RPE-L@uhccvm.uhcc.hawaii.edu**
Moderator's Address: David W. Zuckerman, **dwz2@columbia.edu**, and Daniel Blaine, **daniel@uhunix.uhcc.hawaii.edu**

Topic: Investigating and supporting school restructuring as a means of achieving the goals of public education. RPE-L has been set up by the AERA special interest group on Restructuring Public Education.

SCHOOL-L

Subscription Address: **listserv@irlearn.ucd.ie**
List Address: **SCHOOL-L@irlearn.ucd.ie**
Moderator's Address: Mike Norris, **MNORRIS@irlearn.ucd.ie**

Topic: An e-conference for primary and post-primary schools.

SCHOOL-MANAGEMENT

Subscription Address: **mailbase@mailbase.ac.uk**
List Address: **SCHOOL-MANAGEMENT@mailbase.ac.uk**
Moderator's Address: Mike Fuller, **mff@ukc.ac.uk**

Topic: Education in schools, in particular their management and government and the curriculum. The focus is on British schools.

STASZ1LO

Subscription Address: **listserv@plearn.edu.pl**
List Address: **stasz1lo@plearn.edu.pl**
Moderator's Address: Adam Jmaroz, **JAME@plearn.edu.pl**; Artur Kret, **AKRET@plearn.edu.pl**; and Pawel Gierech, **PGIERECH@plearn.edu.pl**

Topic: Contacts among pupils, teachers, and graduates of Stanislaw Staszic High School (SSHS) in Lublin, Poland, who are interested in exact and technical sciences. Especially encouraged are discussions about mathematics and computer science including usage of computer network in SSHS. The discussion is conducted in Polish (when needed, also English and German).

STWNET

Subscription Address: **majordomo@tristam.edc.org**
List Address: **STWNET@tristam.edc.org**
Moderator's Address: **stw-mod@tristam.edc.org**; Cathy Corbitt, **CathyC@edc.org**; Dr. Joyce Malyn-Smith, **joycem@edc.org**; and Dr. John Wong, **johnw@edc.org**

Topic: Forum on school-to-work (STW) transition, skill standards projects, and the national Youth Fair Chance (YFC) initiative. STWNet welcomes discussion on all STW-related issues, including comprehensive education reform, national skill standards, performance-based education and training programs, workplaces as active learning environments, local partnerships that link the worlds of school and work, YFC initiatives, strategies that assist out-of-school youth, tech-prep, supportive services, and other activities to improve the knowledge and skills of youth by integrating academic and vocational learning. STWNet is a project of Cleveland YFC, funded by the U.S. Department of Labor.

TEACH-L

Subscription Address: **listserv@uicvm.cc.uic.edu**
List Address: **TEACH-L@uicvm.cc.uic.edu**
Moderator's Address: **U29322@uicvm.cc.uic.edu**

Topic: Classroom dynamics.

VOCNET

Subscription Address: **listserv@cmsa.berkeley.edu**
List Address: **VOCNET@cmsa.berkeley.edu**
Moderator's Address: David Carlson, **dcarlson@uclink.berkeley.edu**

Topic: Any aspect of vocational education.

VT-HSNET

Subscription Address: **listserv@vtvm1.cc.vt.edu**
List Address: **VT-HSNET@vtvm1.cc.vt.edu**
Moderator's Address: Phil Benchoff, **BENCHOFF@vtvm1.cc.vt.edu**

Topic: Virginia K-12 School Network.

VRINST-L

Subscription Address: **listserv@uwf.cc.uwf.edu**
List Address: **vrinst-l@uwf.cc.uwf.edu**
Moderator's Address: Pam Taylor Northrup, **PNORTHRU@uwf.cc.uwf.edu**

Topic: Implications of virtual reality for instruction.

WSPLAN

Subscription Address: **listserv@iubvm.ucs.indiana.edu**
List Address: Contact the Moderator
Moderator's Address: **worldsch@ucs.indiana.edu**;
Gerry Sousa, **GSOUSA@ indiana.edu**

Topic: Making education global, relevant, interactive, interdisciplinary, and adventurous for fourth- through ninth-grade students in the United States and in other countries, as well as their teachers. This list is part of the World School for Adventure Learning (WSAL), a nonprofit environmental education program operated by a group of university design partners in the United States: Indiana University's Center for Excellence in Education (Bloomington,

Indiana), the St. Thomas World School (St. Paul, Minnesota), the Center for Global Environment at Hamline University (St. Paul, Minnesota), and Inter-active Communications and Simulations program at the University of Michigan (Ann Arbor, Michigan). The World School incorporates technology and issues-oriented education in order to bring adventure into the classroom and to bring students out of the classroom into adventurous learning. **WSPLAN@iubvm.ucs.indiana.edu** is a listserv devoted to discussions by the teacher design team—a group of teachers worldwide guiding the design of the World School for Adventure Learning.

WVRK12-L

Subscription Address: **listserv@wvnvm.wvnet.edu**
List Address: **WVRK12-L@wvnvm.wvnet.edu**
Moderator's Address: Ermel Stepp, **stepp@marshall.edu**

Topic: Ruralnet Forum on Computer Networking in Education.

WWWEDU

Subscription Address: **listproc@kudzu.cnidr.org**
List Address: **WWWEDU@kudzu.cnidr.org**
Moderator's Address: Andy Carvin, **acarvin@k12.cnidr.org**

Topic: The role of the World Wide Web in education.

Subject-Specific Listservs

The following listservs are meant to help you find colleagues and electronic conferences specific to your discipline.

AERA-F

Subscription Address: **listserv@asuvm.inre.asu.edu**
List Address: **AERA-F@asuvm.inre.asu.edu**
Moderator's Address: Gene V. Glass, **Glass@asu.edu**

Topic: Discussion for AERA Division F: History and Historiography. Sponsored by the American Educational Research Association (AERA) and the College of Education at Arizona State University.

BILINGUE-L

Subscription Address: **listserv@Reynolds.k12.or.us**
List Address: **Bilingue-L@Reynolds.k12.or.us**
Moderator's Address: Lynn Thompson, **Lynn_Thompson@Reynolds.k12.or.us**

Topic: The concerns of elementary teachers of Spanish/English. Issues related to helping Spanish-speaking students become literate in Spanish as well as in English; English-speaking students develop high levels of proficiency in Spanish while making normal progress in English development; both language groups perform academically at their grade level, develop positive attitudes toward both languages and the communities they represent, and develop a positive self-image.

CX-L

Subscription Address: **listserv@uga.cc.uga.edu**
List Address: **cx-l@uga.cc.uga.edu**
Moderator's Address: Doyle Srader **dsrader@uga.cc.uga.edu** or **hootie58@aol.com**

Topic: Discussion and announcements of high school debate.

H-TEACH

Subscription Address: **listserv@H-Net.msu.edu**
List Address: **H-TEACH@H-Net.msu.edu**
Moderator's Address: **hteach@hs1.hst.msu.edu**

Topic: H-Net list for teaching history and related fields.

LITMAG

Subscription Address: **listserv@VM.CC.LATECH.EDU**
List Address: **LITMAG@VM.CC.LATECH.EDU**
Moderator's Address: Eddie Blick, **BLICK@VM.CC.LATECH.EDU**

Topic: Teaching creative writing and/or publishing literary magazines at the high school or junior high school level.

NESS

Subscription Address: **listserv@unl.edu**
List Address: **ness@un1.edu**
Moderator's Address: Linda Price, **pricel@platte.unk.edu** or Daryl Kelley, **kelley@platte.unk.edu**

Topic: General discussion, announcements, information-sharing, and online assistance for social science teachers, instructors, students, and other interested parties.

TEACHMAT

Subscription Address: **listserv@uicvm.cc.uic.edu**
List Address: **TEACHMAT@uicvm.cc.uic.edu**
Moderator's Address: **U12800@uicvm.cc.uic.edu**

Topic: Methods of teaching mathematics.

THINK-L

Subscription Address: **listserv@umslvma.umsl.edu**
List Address: **think-l@umslvma.umsl.edu**
Moderator's Address: **swdklei@umslvma.umsl.edu**

Topic: Critical thinking.

USENET Newsgroups

General Education and Technology Newsgroups

The following academic listservs are meant to provide a starting point for your research into electronic communities. Please read Chapter 4 first if you are unfamiliar with electronic conferences.

misc.education

Subscription Address: Local USENET Newsreader
List Address: **misc.education**

Topic: Educational research, policy, and practice for educators and educational researchers.

k12.chat.teacher

Subscription Address: Local USENET Newsreader
List Address: **k12.chat.teacher**

Topic: Teacher chat. k12.chat* includes many other chat sessions for K-12 folks as well.

Subject-Specific Newsgroups

The following academic listservs are meant to provide a starting point for your research into electronic communities. Please read Chapter 4 first if you are unfamiliar with electronic conferences.

k12.ed.art

Subscription Address: Local USENET Newsreader
List Address: **k12.ed.art**
Moderator's Address: Jack Crawford,
K12Net.Council.(JC)@f620.n260.z1.fidonet.org

Topic: Art education.

k12.ed.business

Subscription Address: Local USENET Newsreader
List Address: **k12.ed.business**

Topic: Business education.

k12.ed.comp.literacy

Subscription Address: Local USENET Newsreader
List Address: **k12.ed.comp.literacy**
Moderator's Address: Terry Bowden, **bowden@sydvm1.vnet.ibm.com**

Topic: Curricular computing.

k12.lang.art

Subscription Address: Local USENET Newsreader
List Address: **k12.lang.art**

Topic: Language arts education. Keywords: Language Arts Education.

k12.ed.math

Subscription Address: Local USENET Newsreader
List Address: **k12.ed.math**

Topic: Math education.

k12.ed.music

Subscription Address: Local USENET Newsreader
List Address: **k12.ed.music**

Topic: Performing Arts Education.

k12.ed.science

Subscription Address: Local USENET Newsreader
List Address: **k12.ed.science**
Moderator's Address: Jack Crawford,
K12Net.Council.(JC)@f620.n260.z1.fidonet.org

Topic: Science education.

k12.ed.soc-studies

Subscription Address: Local USENET Newsreader
List Address: **k12.ed.soc-studies**

Topic: Social studies education.

Foreign Language USENET Groups

These newsgroups deal with foreign language conversation.

k12.lang.esp-eng

Subscription Address: Local USENET Newsreader
List Address: **k12.lang.esp-eng**

Topic: Spanish conversation.

k12.lang.francais

Subscription Address: Local USENET Newsreader
List Address: **k12.lang.francais**
Moderator's Address: Robert Brault

Topic: French conversation.

k12.lang.deutsch-eng

Subscription Address: Local USENET Newsreader
List Address: **k12.lang.deutsch-eng**

Topic: German conversation.

k12.lang.japanese

Subscription Address: Local USENET Newsreader
List Address: **k12.lang.japanese**
Moderator's Address: Terry Bowden, **bowden@sydvm1.vnet.ibm.com**

Topic: Japanese conversation.

k12.lang.russian

Subscription Address: Local USENET Newsreader
List Address: **k12.lang.russian**

Topic: Russian conversation.

Education Resources on the World Wide Web

The following Web sites are meant to help you get started on your searches to find the treasure of information available on the Web. These resources are specific to K-12.

Academy One

Address: http://www.nptn.org:80/cyber.serv/AOneP

Description: Academy One® is an international online educational resource for students, educators, parents, and administrators of grades kindergarten through twelve. It is one of NPTN's three main interactive cybercasting services.

Armadillo's K-12 Resources

Address: http://chico.rice.edu/armadillo/Rice/Resources/reshome.html

Description: This directory of K-12 educational resources has been developed for teachers and students. It is intended to be a list where teachers can quickly access resource materials for direct use in their lesson plans or as additional resources for students to explore.

Blue Web'n

Address: http://www.kn.pacbell.com/wired/bluewebn/#table

Description: This is a very useful site that provides a library of sites, applications, projects, and information. Some of the sites that can be accessed are free, others are not. If a fee is involved, a warning is given ahead of time. An incredibly easy-to-use search engine is provided at the opening page. An absolute must for anyone using the Net to teach.

Bread Loaf School of English Educational Technology Page

Address: http://tigger.clemson.edu/bnet/resources/edtech.html

Description: An excellent education resource on the Web. Links to Big Sky Language Arts Lesson Plans, the Clearinghouse on Reading, English and Communication Exemplary Lesson Plans, ERIC Lesson Plans, and Houghton Mifflin's Activity Search are included.

Classroom Connect

Address: http://www.classroom.net

Description: A commercial site dedicated to K-12 educators, students, and resources.

CO-NECT SCHOOLS Home Page

Address: http://co-nect.bbn.com

Description: An interesting project that's trying to connect students with teachers from around the country to promote math, science, and problem solving. As of this writing, there were openings for 100 teachers and 600 students. Anyone wanting to join this "school" should visit the site where a complete history and detailed information is available. This project could turn out to be very interesting.

The EdWeb Home Room

Address: http://k12.cnidr.org:90/resource.cntnts.html

Description: One of the Web's best K-12 sites! Links to general education information, help with HTML, and K-12 resources are included. The K-12 resources link is truly extensive and includes teacher discussion groups and administrative services, as well as lesson plans, interactive projects, and interesting places for kids to explore.

Global SchoolNet Foundation

Address: http://www.gsn.org

Description: A very interesting site to visit. A lot of information and tips on how to use the Internet in the classroom, K-12 projects, and electronic mailing lists can be found here. Definitely a place to visit on a regular basis.

Global Web Site Project

Address: http://wolfen.wolfe.k12.ky.us/globe/globe.htm

Description: Recently started by Russell Halsey, Director of Technology Services for Wolfe County Public Schools located in Wolfe County, Kentucky, the site is to be used to provide educational and cultural exchange experiences for students worldwide.

History/Social Studies Web Site for K-12 Teachers

Address: http://www.execpc.com/~dboals/boals.html

Description: A site designed to encourage the use of the World Wide Web as a learning tool and forum for teaching. The site provides extensive links to help teachers locate resources available on the Internet.

Index of /Edu/Classroom

Address: http://www.ncsa.uiuc.edu/Edu/Classroom

Description: A gopher-like menu of information compiled by the Education & Outreach Division of the NCSA (National Center for Supercomputing Association), the site provides links to a variety of sources related to K-12 education.

Institute for Technology and Learning at the University of Texas at Austin

Address: http://www.ital.utexas.edu

Description: ITAL's mission is to "identify, design, create, and disseminate high-quality, computer-based instructional materials for students and teachers in grades K-12." The site lives up to its mission and is well worth taking the time to visit.

Kids Web: A World Wide Web Digital Library for Schoolkids

Address: http://www.npac.syr.edu/textbook/kidsweb

Description: A terrific starting place for teachers and kids to find information about every subject. Organized by topic categories, this site is a must for anyone interested in using multimedia resources in the classroom.

K-12 Education Resources

Address: http://www.nceet.snre.umich.edu/listEd.html

Description: Maintained by the University of Michigan, this site is a gold mine of practical information. The site contains links to lesson plans, sites for kids, classroom activities, and more.

LiveText Educational Resources: "The Home Page for K12 Education"

Address: http://www.ilt.columbia.edu/k12/livetext

Description: LiveText is a comprehensive, annotated, structured index to online resources relating to network technologies and their use in K-12 schools.

Mathematic Archives—K12 Internet Sites

Address: http://archives.math.utk.edu/k12.html

Description: An extensive archive of resources from AIMS Education Foundation to Weights and Measures. You'll find Ask Dr. Math, Activities for Integrating Math and Science, and many additional links.

MathMagic

Address: http://forum.swarthmore.edu/mathmagic/what.html

Description: MathMagic is a K-12 telecommunications project developed in El Paso, Texas. It provides strong motivation for students to use computer technology while increasing problem-solving strategies and communications skills.

NickNacks

Address: http://www1.minn.net:80/~schubert/NickNacks.html

Description: Maintained by Nancy Schubert, this site is terrific for information about how to create your own collaborative Internet learning projects.

Sally Laughon, Ph.D. to be! Page

Address: http://infoserver.etl.vt.edu/~/Laughon/Sally_p.html

Description: A terrific collection of K-12 project links. Visit it soon, as it might disappear in the near future.

St. Olaf's Gopher Menu

Address: gopher://gopher.stolaf.edu:70/1m/Internet%20Resources/ St.%20Olaf%20Sponsored%20Mailing%20Lists/Intercultural-Email- Classroom-Connections/archive.projects

Description: This gopher site is an excellent starting place for teachers who are unfamiliar with, or just a little nervous about, using the Internet in the classroom. It is also a first-rate example of the kinds of projects that are possible for use in the classroom with the Internet. I would recommend that all teachers visit this site. You won't regret the time spent.

Schools of Distinction on the Web

Address: http://199.233.193.1/schools.html

Description: This site is a listing of schools on the Internet, K-12. This listing includes the U.K., Germany, Australia, Europe, Canada, and the U.S. It also lists some of the national and international organizations that are supporting schools on the Internet. An excellent source for making contacts in case one wants to look for specific areas of the world to conduct projects.

Teaching with Electronic Technology

Address: http://www.wam.umd.edu/~mlhall/teaching.html

Description: An excellent resource page housed at the University of Maryland with links to information about conferences and publications, and examples of electronic resources.

Technology Based Learning Network Canada (TBL.CA) Home Page

Address: http://www.humanities.mcmaster.ca/~misc2/tblca1.htm

Description: Another excellent starting point for research into uses of technology in the K-12 classroom with links to other resources in the U.S. and Canada.

Technology and Education Resources: Projects

Address: http://odysseus.calumet.yorku.ca/courses/sourcelists/EdRes/ EdTech.html#projects

Description: A list of established education projects, mostly from the U.K., U.S., Australia, and Canada.

A Gallery of Projects on the World Wide Web

The following pages contain photos of some excellent work by K-12 students and teachers from across the world. I hope these inspire you and get your imagination churning. Enjoy!

Mendocino Bird Research Project
Address: http://www.mms.mendocino.k12.ca.us/gs/ca/jm

Description: A very good example of a first and second grade teacher using the Internet in a different way that first and second graders will find useful. An interesting, collaborative project.

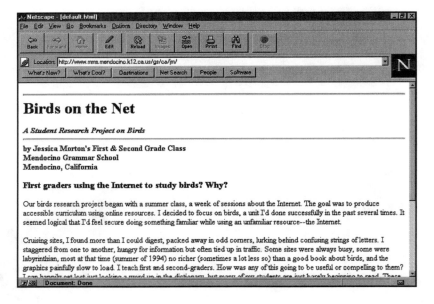

Fig. D.1   Birds on the Net.

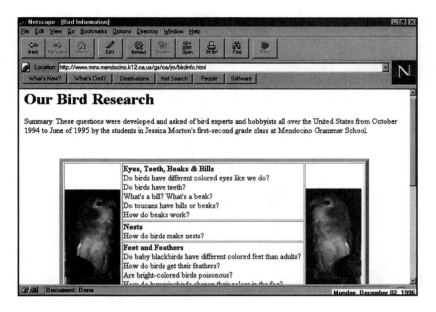

Fig. D.2 Birds on the Net.

Arbor Heights Elementary School Site
Address: http://www.halcyon.com/arborhts/arborhts.html

Description: Created by Arbor Heights Elementary school in Seattle, Washington, this site is a good example of what can be accomplished using Internet resources. This is also a good place for elementary kids who like to write to see what other elementary kids are doing.

Frontier School Internet Science Room
Address: http://pc65.frontier.osrhe.edu/hs/science/hsci.htm

Description: This is an active Web site that encourages high school students to take more responsibility for their own education in the sciences. It provides links that utilize databases so that the students can do their own research and process that information as to relative value and importance that it has concerning their project. It also provides the student with the ability to set up a virtual lab to test their hypothesis. This is a must-see for all high school students taking science classes!

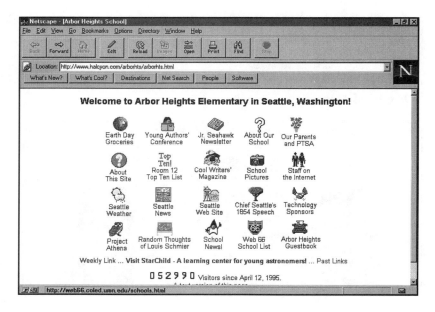

Fig. D.3 Arbor Heights Elementary School.

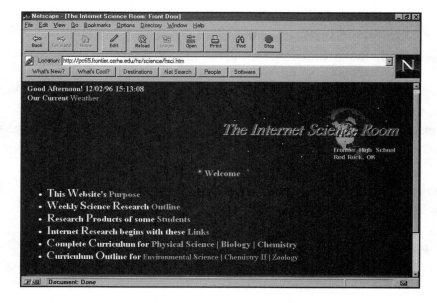

Fig. D.4 The Internet Science Room.

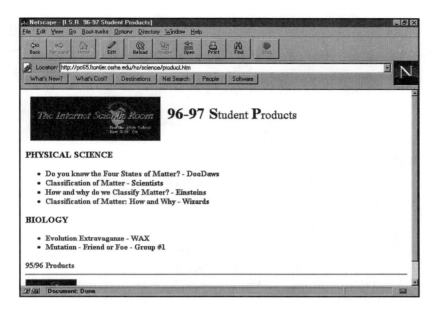

Fig. D.5 The Internet Science Room.

"Monsters, Monsters, Monsters"
Address: http://www.coedu.usf.edu/inst_tech/students/gerzoge/index.html

Description: The purpose of Monsters, Monsters, Monsters is to introduce primary and early childhood students to the concepts of the Internet, telecommunications, and e-mail. For teachers, the project has the purpose of teaching them how to incorporate telecommunications into their existing curriculum and into classroom instruction.

"The Prison Project"
Address: http://168.216.210.13/mjhs/pproject/pproject.htm

Description: Student discussions with prison inmates. An innovative and thought-provoking middle school project with far-reaching social import, from Bill Burrall, computer instructor at Moundsville Junior High, Moundsville, W.V. The kind of project we'd all like to design!

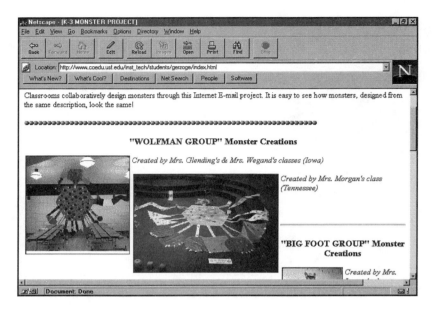

Fig. D.6   Monsters!

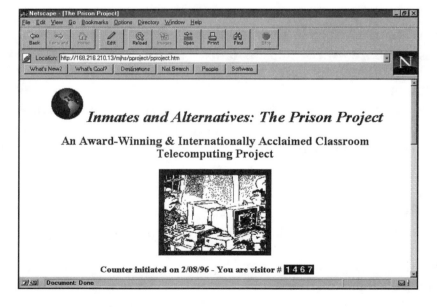

Fig. D.7   The Prison Project.

"Graph Your Favorite"

Address: http://www1.minn.net:80/~schubert/Graph.html

Description: Grade 2, 4, and 6 classes exchanged, compiled, and analyzed data on their favorite pets, sports, foods, and school subjects.

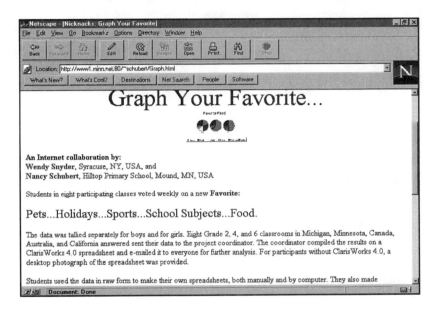

Fig. D.8 Kids' Graphs.

"Who Elects the President?"

Address: http://www1.minn.net:80/~schubert/VoteOv.html

Description: Research, voting, data analysis, discussion, and writing. Students in grades 5-12 research the Election '96 Presidential candidates and issues, and consider voting issues in online editorials and political cartoons.

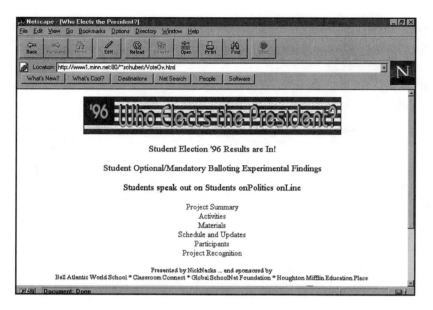

Fig. D.9 Electioneers.

Taking Stock
Address: http://www.santacruz.k12.ca.us/~jpost/projects/TS/TS.html

Description: Taking Stock is a multi-grade project focusing on the stock market with participants in grades 5 through 12 from California to New York to Florida.

Mega-Mathematics
Address: http://www.c3.lanl.gov/mega-math/

Description: A "must-see" site for mathematics and science teachers.

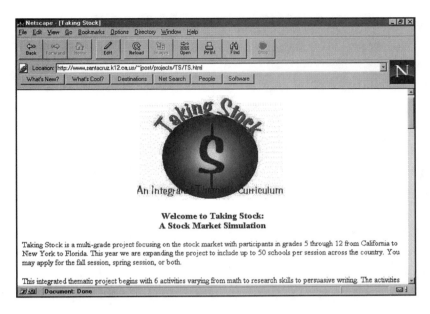

Fig. D.10 Taking Stock.

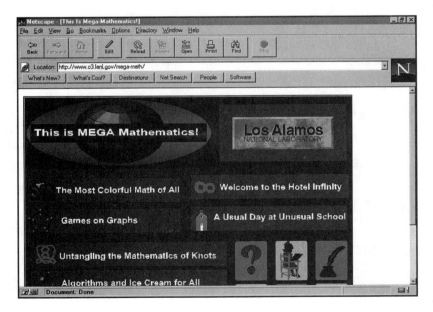

Fig. D.11 Mega-Mathematics.

Index

M

Check out Que® Books on the World Wide Web
http://www.mcp.com/que

As the biggest software release in computer history, Windows 95 continues to redefine the computer industry. Click here for the latest info on our Windows 95 books

Make computing quick and easy with these products designed exclusively for new and casual users

Examine the latest releases in word processing, spreadsheets, operating systems, and suites

The Internet, The World Wide Web, CompuServe®, America Online®, Prodigy® —it's a world of ever-changing information. Don't get left behind!

Find out about new additions to our site, new bestsellers and hot topics

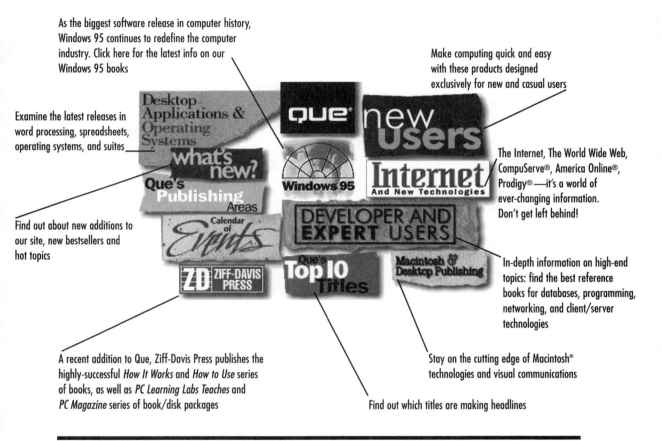

In-depth information on high-end topics: find the best reference books for databases, programming, networking, and client/server technologies

A recent addition to Que, Ziff-Davis Press publishes the highly-successful *How It Works* and *How to Use* series of books, as well as *PC Learning Labs Teaches* and *PC Magazine* series of book/disk packages

Stay on the cutting edge of Macintosh® technologies and visual communications

Find out which titles are making headlines

With 6 separate publishing groups, Que develops products for many specific market segments and areas of computer technology. Explore our Web Site and you'll find information on best-selling titles, newly published titles, upcoming products, authors, and much more.

- Stay informed on the latest industry trends and products available
- Visit our online bookstore for the latest information and editions
- Download software from Que's library of the best shareware and freeware

QUE® has the right choice for every computer user

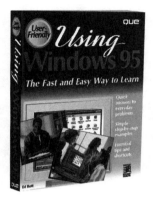

From the new computer user to the advanced programmer, we've got the right computer book for you. Our user-friendly *Using* series offers just the information you need to perform specific tasks quickly and move onto other things. And, for computer users ready to advance to new levels, QUE *Special Edition Using* books, the perfect all-in-one resource—and recognized authority on detailed reference information.

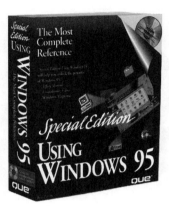

The *Using* series for casual users	*Special Edition Using* for accomplished users
Who should use this book?	**Who should use this book?**
Everyday users who:	Proficient computer users who:
• Work with computers in the office or at home	• Have a more technical understanding of computers
• Are familiar with computers but not in love with technology	• Are interested in technological trends
• Just want to "get the job done"	• Want in-depth reference information
• Don't want to read a lot of material	• Prefer more detailed explanations and examples
The user-friendly reference	**The most complete reference**
• The fastest access to the one best way to get things done	• Thorough explanations of various ways to perform tasks
• Bite-sized information for quick and easy reference	• In-depth coverage of all topics
• Nontechnical approach in plain English	• Technical information cross-referenced for easy access
• Real-world analogies to explain new concepts	• Professional tips, tricks, and shortcuts for experienced users
• Troubleshooting tips to help solve problems	• Advanced troubleshooting information with alternative approaches
• Visual elements and screen pictures that reinforce topics	• Visual elements and screen pictures that reinforce topics
• Expert authors who are experienced in training and instruction	• Technically qualified authors who are experts in their fields
	• "Techniques from the Pros" sections with advice from well-known computer professionals

Complete and Return this Card
for a *FREE* Computer Book Catalog

Thank you for purchasing this book! You have purchased a superior computer book written expressly for your needs. To continue to provide the kind of up-to-date, pertinent coverage you've come to expect from us, we need to hear from you. Please take a minute to complete and return this self-addressed, postage-paid form. In return, we'll send you a free catalog of all our computer books on topics ranging from word processing to programming and the internet.

:. ☐   Mrs. ☐   Ms. ☐   Dr. ☐

me (first) ⬚⬚⬚⬚⬚⬚⬚⬚⬚⬚⬚ (M.I.) ☐   (last) ⬚⬚⬚⬚⬚⬚⬚⬚⬚⬚⬚⬚⬚⬚⬚

ddress ⬚⬚⬚⬚⬚⬚⬚⬚⬚⬚⬚⬚⬚⬚⬚⬚⬚⬚⬚⬚⬚⬚⬚⬚⬚⬚

⬚⬚⬚⬚⬚⬚⬚⬚⬚⬚⬚⬚⬚⬚⬚⬚⬚⬚⬚⬚⬚⬚⬚⬚⬚⬚

ty ⬚⬚⬚⬚⬚⬚⬚⬚⬚⬚⬚⬚⬚⬚   State ⬚⬚   Zip ⬚⬚⬚⬚⬚ ⬚⬚⬚⬚

one ⬚⬚⬚ ⬚⬚⬚ ⬚⬚⬚⬚   Fax ⬚⬚⬚ ⬚⬚⬚ ⬚⬚⬚⬚

mpany Name ⬚⬚⬚⬚⬚⬚⬚⬚⬚⬚⬚⬚⬚⬚⬚⬚⬚⬚⬚⬚⬚⬚⬚⬚

mail address ⬚⬚⬚⬚⬚⬚⬚⬚⬚⬚⬚⬚⬚⬚⬚⬚⬚⬚⬚⬚⬚⬚⬚⬚

Please check at least (3) influencing factors for purchasing this book.

ont or back cover information on book .... ☐
ecial approach to the content .... ☐
mpleteness of content .... ☐
thor's reputation .... ☐
blisher's reputation .... ☐
ok cover design or layout .... ☐
lex or table of contents of book .... ☐
ice of book .... ☐
ecial effects, graphics, illustrations .... ☐
her (Please specify): _____ ☐

How did you first learn about this book?

w in Macmillan Computer Publishing catalog .... ☐
commended by store personnel .... ☐
w the book on bookshelf at store .... ☐
commended by a friend .... ☐
ceived advertisement in the mail .... ☐
w an advertisement in: _____ ☐
ad book review in: _____ ☐
her (Please specify): _____ ☐

How many computer books have you purchased in the last six months?

is book only .... ☐   3 to 5 books .... ☐
ooks .... ☐   More than 5 .... ☐

4. Where did you purchase this book?

Bookstore .... ☐
Computer Store .... ☐
Consumer Electronics Store .... ☐
Department Store .... ☐
Office Club .... ☐
Warehouse Club .... ☐
Mail Order .... ☐
Direct from Publisher .... ☐
Internet site .... ☐
Other (Please specify): _____ ☐

5. How long have you been using a computer?

☐ Less than 6 months   ☐ 6 months to a year
☐ 1 to 3 years   ☐ More than 3 years

6. What is your level of experience with personal computers and with the subject of this book?

	With PCs	With subject of book
New	☐	☐
Casual	☐	☐
Accomplished	☐	☐
Expert	☐	☐

Source Code ISBN: 0-7897-1045-5

7. Which of the following best describes your job title?

Administrative Assistant .... ☐
Coordinator .... ☐
Manager/Supervisor .... ☐
Director .... ☐
Vice President .... ☐
President/CEO/COO .... ☐
Lawyer/Doctor/Medical Professional .... ☐
Teacher/Educator/Trainer .... ☐
Engineer/Technician .... ☐
Consultant .... ☐
Not employed/Student/Retired .... ☐
Other (Please specify): _____ ☐

8. Which of the following best describes the area of the company your job title falls under?

Accounting .... ☐
Engineering .... ☐
Manufacturing .... ☐
Operations .... ☐
Marketing .... ☐
Sales .... ☐
Other (Please specify): _____ ☐

9. What is your age?

Under 20 .... ☐
21-29 .... ☐
30-39 .... ☐
40-49 .... ☐
50-59 .... ☐
60-over .... ☐

10. Are you:

Male .... ☐
Female .... ☐

11. Which computer publications do you read regularly? (Please list)

_____
_____
_____
_____
_____
_____
_____
_____
_____
_____

Comments: _____
_____
_____

Fold here and scotch-tape to ma

MACMILLAN COMPUTER PUBLISHING USA

A VIACOM COMPANY

Technical ---- Support:

If you need assistance with the information in this book or with a CD/Disk accompanying the book, please access the Knowledge Base on our Web site at **http://www.superlibrary.com/general/support**. Our most Frequently Asked Questions are answered there. If you do not find the answer to your questions on our Web site, you may contact Macmillan Technical Support **(317) 581-3833** or e-mail us at **support@mcp.com**.